Patricia Bartlett
and Ernie Wagner

Pythons

Everything About Purchase,
Care, Nutrition, and Behavior

BARRON'S

2 C O N T E N T S

ABOUT PYTHONS

Pythons are relatively primitive snakes belonging to the family Pythonidae.

Pythonidae, in turn, is contained within the suborder *Serpentes*, the snakes. Family members share some common characteristics, including two lungs (most snakes only have one), constriction of prey, and cloacal spurs. Pythons also have another intriguing characteristic: heat-sensing areas on their snout and lips which make them quite good at nailing their warm-blooded prey (or the human who is annoying them).

Pythons range in size from very big (the Burmese and reticulated pythons can grow to 20 feet-plus and over 200 lbs), to small (the Children's python doesn't get much bigger than 24 inches in length).

Pythons are restricted in their native range to parts of the world most of us only dream about: Africa, Asia, and Australia and in Indo-

This adult green tree python from the Wamena locale is poised for striking.

Philippine Islands. Due to human foibles (a nice word for short-sighted stupidity), at least one python has recently become established in the United States—the Burmese python in Florida's Everglades. Although many herp hobbyists view snake-watching as a specialized type of tourism, no one in Florida finds the introduced Burmese as anything but a huge liability. Snake hunters have been hired to seek out and destroy any Burmese they find.

But let's talk about pythons in general and what makes them so spectacular. First of all, a few words on how python species are named and why this process is important.

Binomial Nomenclature

The original system of classification, called binomial nomenclature, was designed by Carl von Linne in 1756. The system identifies plants and animals by two names, and it uses physical

Taxonomy

Kingdom	Animalia (all animals, from amoebas to humans)
Phylum	Chordata (animals with notocords, a form of spinal cord)
Subphylum	Vertebrata (animals with backbones)
Class	Reptilia (all reptiles)
Order	Squamata (possessing scales—the snakes and lizards)
Suborder	Serpentes (all snakes, some 3,000 kinds)
Family	Pythonidae (pythons)
Genus	*Morelia* (one of 11 species within the subfamily)
Species	*viridis* (one of the six species within the genus)

similarities to group animals or plants by increasingly rigid criteria. Snakes are grouped together, and as the criteria get more selective, snakes of similar appearances and habits are grouped together.

Within the family of pythons, arboreal pythons (green tree pythons) are grouped separately from terrestrial pythons with heavy bodies and short tails (blood pythons). Each different type of snake eventually ends up with two names, the first for the genus and the second for the species. When isolated populations exist which are still identifiable as the same type of snake, a third name, the trinomial, is added.

The term "primitive" indicates that these snakes were some of the first snakes to evolve. Primitive snakes display features which link them to lizards. These features include a rudimentary pelvic girdle, cloacal spurs, and lungs of equal sizes. Advanced snakes, like the rat snakes and whip snakes, have only one functional lung, and have no cloacal spurs.

Pythons are divided into about 26 species, depending on which authority you accept (like other fields, different researchers are most emphatic that their own criteria represent the best way to define the species).

But using only physical characteristics to describe animals' relationships to each other went out the window when we found we could compare DNA. The light bulb went off in a 500-watt flash as we realized we could actually define and compare animals by their chemical makeup. The downside was that DNA analysis takes time and expensive machinery. So for now, we're in an uneasy marriage of DNA and readily discernible physical characteristics, and we still can't agree on what's more important. If past trends are any indication, new divisions and re-definitions will continue to be issued, compared, and criticized. They may even be accepted—for a while.

Python Reproduction

Pythons are oviparous; the eggs are surrounded by a thin, parchment-like shell. Females of most species of pythons will coil around their eggs and stay with them during the incubation period. A couple of species are actually able to generate heat through continuous body contractions and so help the incubation process by raising their own temperature, and consequently the temperature of the eggs.

Although still frequently offered as the "African burrowing python," **Calabaria reinhardtii** *is now thought to be a sand boa.*

When this behavior was first described, the observations were not unilaterally accepted. When the babies hatch, they cut a slit through the egg shell with an egg tooth on the tip of their nose and crawl out.

Python eggs take about two months to hatch and the eggs seem to have more specific temperature requirements than other snake eggs. Python eggs incubated at inadequate temperatures will result in large numbers of stillbirths and birth defects such as spinal kyphosis (backward curvature of the spine) or incomplete development. Oddly enough, when the incubation temperature is too low, you will also frequently see anomalies in the pattern, such as striping. Be aware that if you're offered an unusually striped specimen, the pattern may be the result of incubation temperatures and not genetics—but you'd ask about the genetics behind an unusual color or pattern morph anyway, wouldn't you?

Python life span, like most snakes, averages 20 to 25 years. But a snake kept under good conditions may live a lot longer than that—a ball python in the Highland Park Zoo in Pennsylvania lived for 47 years! When you buy a python, it ought to live for a long time.

Pythons are found in a wide variety of environments, from very humid and wet to very dry. Although pythons have found ways to survive in very hot climates (nocturnal activity is one of them), their geographic range is circumscribed by low temperatures.

Even among the normal-colored ball pythons, as displayed by these three, there may be considerable variation in pattern.

Habitat

With the exception of one or two relatively small arboreal species, most pythons are ground dwellers, living in burrows or under some kind of ground shelter, occasionally basking in the daytime but doing most of their hunting at night. During extremely hot and dry conditions, some species will go underground and become inactive until conditions change. With most, the climatic change which triggers reproduction is the onset of cooler temperatures.

Endangered Status

Many species of pythons are endangered in their native countries. The loss of habitat is the main reason. Habitat destruction is also a serious threat to the long-term survival of many non-reptilian species.

The skin trade and humans hunting for food (in some cultures, protein is wherever you can find it) have also taken their toll. The pet trade consumes large numbers of one or two species, such as the African ball python.

While the numbers of pythons which are legally imported are monitored by CITES, the Convention in Trade Endangered Species, the care of these animals is not. Conditions under which the animals are held and eventually shipped often lead to disease and mortality. Wholesalers are dealing in numbers, not in captive care techniques.

Captive-bred Young

Not all pythons must be caught in the wild and imported to reach your local pet dealer. Many python species, including the endangered

This is a naturally occurring intergrade (hybrid) of an inland carpet python and a diamond python.

ones, are available from captive breeders. The shorthand term for these snakes is "cb/ch," meaning "captive bred and captive hatched." It's obvious that a cb/ch animal is more accustomed to captivity than its wild-caught counterpart. There's another plus which isn't apparent until you bring the animal home and begin to work with it: captive-borns are much calmer and less inclined to bite than adults or young from the wild. Captive-born animals are also accustomed to the foods offered by their keepers. Legalities aside, an olive python which has been feeding on young wallabies in the wild may not find even the fluffiest rabbit appetizing, and scenting the unfamiliar food item with the python's preferred prey is going to be difficult.

The source of your potential pet python and the characteristics of the species should both be considered in deciding what python you want. Research the qualities of the pythons that appeal to you beforehand, including their temperament. Keep in mind that some python species get too large to handle safely. Some are calm, docile creatures who seem to recognize their keeper. Other species never get out of the habit of striking at any human—or even worse, some can be calm and collected at one moment and then lunge for you the next. Different geographic populations of the same species of python may be calmer, easier to feed, or may grow larger. New information about python behavior is made available on a regular basis online, in reptile magazines, journals, and in reptile club newsletters. Both you and your python will benefit from your education.

UNDERSTANDING YOUR PYTHON

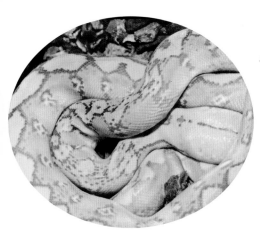

Pythons are ideal pets in many ways. They are quiet, easy to care for, and can be left for a week's vacation with a "sitter." Despite these "carefree" features, there are some special considerations when choosing to live with a python.

Before You Buy a Python

You'll be together for a long time. Remember this is a long-lived pet, certainly up to 20 years or more, far longer than a cat or a dog. As with a dog or a cat, you must be ready to take care of your python throughout its long life.

Size and Feeding

Snakes are guided by instinct, and one of those instincts tells a snake that when it smells food and something in the area is moving, the moving object is prey. A big snake is a strong

The smallest of the pythons, the anthill python may be adult at only 2 feet in total length.

snake. People have actually been killed by their large pet pythons by making mistakes at feeding time. Having said that, we need to remind you that thousands of large pythons are kept as pets all over the country, and in the last 10 years there have been only about half a dozen documented python-related deaths.

Consider Adult Size: Pythons are constrictors. They tightly hold their prey in their coils until the animal suffocates. Some pythons get big; depending on the species, a python can certainly grow to 20 feet and weigh more than most grown men. A snake of 10 feet or more is a strong snake, and takes special consideration in housing, feeding, and handling. ONE person cannot safely handle a python larger than 10 feet, no matter what kind it is.

A relatively inexpensive giant python, the African rock python often has an irascible disposition and is a poor choice as a pet snake.

In addition to adult size, another consideration is food. Large pythons are generally fed rabbits. Do you want to offer these gentle, doe-eyed creatures to your snake? You *can* obtain frozen rabbits, thaw them in warm water and then feed them to your snake, but the process is time-consuming. Many people find the prospect of storing a couple of frozen rabbits next to the frozen peas depressing, and the aspect of buying and killing live rabbits is no better. (Veteran snake keepers use prekilled prey for all their snakes; see Chapter 4 for why this is important.)

There are, however, several species of attractive, good-natured pythons with an adult size of four feet or less which will happily eat prekilled mice or rats.

Consider temperament: Are you interested in a pet that is gentle and easy to handle, or are you more interested in a colorful snake which may be bad-tempered but makes a beautiful or impressive display? Ball, Children's, blotched, and Stimson's pythons are easy-going, small-sized pythons that generally do well in captivity (of course there are caveats; see the species accounts for these). White-lips, chondros, and Burmese pythons are showy creatures, but see the species accounts for the think-twice caveats.

Consider getting bitten: Every hobbyist has his or her favorite story about getting bitten. Generally any conversation that deals with

The Law, You, and Your Python

To check the legalities of specific species, call your municipal government, your state game commission, or the Department of the Interior.

getting bitten is punctuated with high hilarity, because eventually all snake keepers get bitten. ("There I was, my nose bitten and both of my thumbs in the snake's mouth, and all Fred could do was laugh!") Bites can be serious business, though, and here's why:

Pythons have anywhere from 100 to 150 teeth in their mouth, and the teeth in the front are longer than the teeth in the back. When it comes to feeding, a python's survival depends on its ability to snag and hold onto prey items using only its teeth and coils.

But sometimes the bite is out of fear, or is an indication of territorial aggression. A fearful python tends to bite and then loosely hold on. Any motion on your part simply pulls the teeth through the wound and makes the wound larger. The wound size is largely determined by the size of the teeth. The larger the python, the bigger the teeth; for a 12-footer, you're dealing with teeth a half-inch long. A bite from a snake longer than 6 feet can mean a visit to the emergency room of your local hospital, stitches, shots, and a lot of attention you'd rather not have.

A bite from a hatchling or small adult python of five feet or so is usually not a big deal. Wash the affected area and apply a light compress to stop the bleeding. If any of the snake's teeth are left in the wound, remove them. Keep the area dry and clean until the cuts are completely closed. Bandage the area to keep it clean until it heals, but keep an eye on it to make sure there are no signs of infection.

Precise striping has been developed in reticulated pythons, a species normally having a complex pattern of saddles.

The Law, Your Python, and You

There was a time just a few years ago when, if a hobbyist wanted and could afford a big python, he or she could simply go out and buy the big snake. In some areas this is still the case, but in many municipalities the ownership of snakes—especially the larger python species—is becoming increasingly regulated.

Because the regulations are so varied, we will make no effort to provide specifics, but here are examples of a few of the laws and regulations that may be encountered:

1. Total prohibition: The keeping of all snakes may be made illegal by statewide or municipal decrees.

2. Specified species are prohibited: Prohibitions may apply and are often directed (but are not necessarily limited) to non-indigenous snake species, protected snake species, venomous snake species, or large constrictors.

3. Species over a certain length when adult are prohibited.

4. Licenses are required for certain species: Annual licensing fees may vary from $5 to more than $100 and are often required for venomous snakes, non-indigenous snakes, or giant snakes.

5. Licenses are required for all species: Seemingly self-explanatory, the issuance of licenses may be as simple as a cash transaction or as complex as requiring that a specified number of hours of handling experience be documented before a hobbyist is eligible for ownership of certain snake species.

6. Microchipping may be required for snakes of specified species or those over a specified weight, length, or diameter.

7. Caging types and construction parameters may be specified. Cages for large pythons may need to be stronger, more secure, and have locking lids and/or doors.

8. Transportation laws: Laws that apply to the shipping of reptiles may restrict what can be shipped (the U.S. Postal Service, for instance, forbids the shipping of snakes of any size or species by mail). Interstate sales of endangered species will require a federal permit. Intrastate sales normally require no permit. Illegal interstate sales (including shipping methods) may invoke a federal provision known as the Lacey Act.

The python species most often affected by the various laws and regulations are the giant species: the Burmese python, the reticulated python, the African rock python, and the amethystine python. The regulations usually apply to the "dwarfed forms" of the affected species, as well as those of normal size.

There are other reasons why you do not want the snake to bite you. If you jerk your hand away when you get bitten, you'll probably jerk out some of the snake's teeth, which opens the doors to mouth rot (for the snake—not you). Secondly, if a snake bites you and you overreact and drop the snake, severe and largely undetectable abdominal and vertebral damage can result. Many python species never leave ground level, and are completely incapable of falling without incurring damage. And for obvious reasons, do not let a friend handle your python unless you

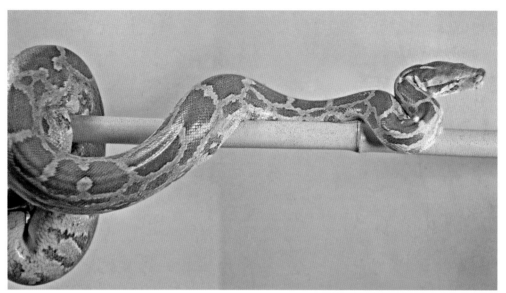

Some municipalities outlaw the keeping of snakes with the growth potential of the Indian rock python.

are there and are absolutely certain of the friend and the snake. Friendships can be lost over things like python bites and injured snakes.

Legal considerations need to be a factor when choosing a pet python. Many states and local municipalities have laws restricting the keeping of snakes over a certain size. If you are purchasing your snake from a local pet shop, the shop employees should—**should**—tell you about local size restrictions. Keep in mind that most pet shops have a no-return policy on live animals and will not refund the purchase price, no matter what your reason for the return.

Where to Get Your Python

Buy captive-bred (termed "cb"), captive-hatched ("ch") pythons over wild-caught ("wc")

animals. In addition to the decreased pressure on wild populations, there are some very practical and economic reasons for this choice. Captive-bred animals will usually be free of parasites and less stressed than wild caught animals. They are more accustomed to easily obtained food; ball pythons from the wild, for instance, are famous for being picky eaters. In contrast, a captive-born baby ball python will present none of these feeding problems.

Many pet stores offer only cb/ch pythons, and for some species which are protected in their country of origin, this is the only way they are available. If your local pet store does not have the kind of python you are looking for, try your local herpetological society or attend a reptile expo. The display and classified ads in a reptile magazine may also offer pythons.

Pythons, both common and rare, may be offered at herp expos across the world.

If you buy your snake from a local source, handle the snake yourself before you buy it. Look for any problems such as wheezing, body lumps, parasites, or contusions. Find out what the snake has been eating, and how recently it has fed.

Buying from a dealer is a more little complex, but not overwhelmingly so. Dealers list their snakes with online services such as *kingsnake.com*, or they send out e-mail lists of their available species. All you need to do is to spend a few minutes reading the lists. Sex is indicated by numbers; 1.2.5 indicates one male, two females, and five yet-to-be sexed snakes. Dealers usually add notes on the size and any special notes ("the prettiest we've EVER seen!" is typical hype).

If you find a python of the species, size, sex, color morph, and price you like, contact the dealer and let him or her know you're interested in that particular snake. Ask if it is feeding, what it feeds on, and talk about the price, payment method, and shipping arrangements. The price is rarely negotiable unless you're very good friends with the wholesaler, or unless there's something very wrong with the snake. A wholesaler doesn't want to sell you a sick snake, but maybe the snake you want is missing its tail tip or is scarred from a recent encounter with another python. Maybe the dealer thinks that python is gravid, reason for extra caution in shipping and an increase in price.

Payment Modes

Reptile dealers deal in cash or in credit cards. A money order, cashier's check, or wire transfer of funds is the same as cash, for most dealers. If a dealer will accept your personal check, expect a week or so delay while the check clears the bank.

Shipping

Dealers ship one or two days a week. Keep in mind that the shipping charges will be added to the price of the snake, so that $300 python will actually cost you a minimum of $350.

Your supplier will ask you details on shipping, or will ask you to go online to fill out a form. Door-to-door freight services such as FedEx or DHL make shipping simple and much faster than dealing with airline air freight offices. Do ask for the tracking number for the shipment—it's how you'll track down your shipment should the package go astray (rare, but it happens).

Expect your shipment to take about 24 hours from the time your dealer ships it to you to the time it arrives at your doorstep. If you work during the week, ask your shipper to ship to you on Friday, so you'll be home on Saturday to receive the package. You can also make arrangements with the shipping firm about leaving the package in a sheltered, secure spot at your home, perhaps on a side porch.

If there's a problem: Reliable dealers guarantee live delivery. If there is a discrepancy, both the dealer and the transport company will want you to fill out a claim report. Be sure to contact the dealer immediately about the problem.

Pretty when photographed as a young adult, with advancing age a suffusion of melanin caused this male jungle carpet python to turn almost entirely black.

Behavior Notes

When you open the bag: Although many pythons will allow gentle handling, go slowly. Your python will be shipped in a bag within a Styrofoam box. When you open the bag, reach in and grasp your snake, gently and slowly. Inspect the snake for obvious problems such as ticks, mites, or physical damage. Place the snake in its cage, close the cage, and leave it alone for a few hours. Give the snake time to adjust to the new smells, lighting, and temperature of its cage.

When you open the cage, don't yank the door open and grab for the snake. Move slowly and deliberately. There is only one way for your snake to protest, and that's with its mouth. Some snakes will never adjust to being handled, and will protest these overtures on your part. These pythons include the Macklot's and white-lipped pythons and the African rock python. They may need to be considered display animals only, and, while their size permits (the rock pythons get big), they can be moved and manipulated on a snake hook.

CAGING

What kind of caging you can provide in terms of space and materials plays an important role in the selection of your pet python and how well your python will do in captivity.

Cage materials can range from simple, using an aquarium tank as a terrarium, to home-made, creating basically a glass-fronted box, to commercial units, made from fiberglass or mica laminate.

What to provide: You'll need to provide enough space for the snake, a hiding area, a water bowl, and a heating/lighting source that will heat a basking area to about 90–93°F (33–34°C). Arboreal species will need climbing limbs.

How big? While you're thinking about possible materials, think about space—of the cage itself and how much room you can devote to a cage. As far as the snake is concerned, the overall length of the cage should be roughly

Albino ball pythons are attractive, available, and expensive.

$^2/_3$ the snake's length; cage width can be a little less, perhaps $^1/_2$ the length of your snake. There is room for adjustment in these figures; the goal is to give the snake enough room to turn around easily.

But don't forget that some pythons get big, very big. As your snake matures, the cage size needs to increase as well. A Children's or Savu python, which matures at three feet, needs a cage at least 24 inches long by 12 inches deep, or the standard 20-gallon aquarium size. An adult snake as large as a Burmese will require a room-sized enclosure.

Local and state regulations need to be considered. Your state may have a minimum cage size, based on the length of the snake. In Florida, for instance, the perimeter measurement of the cage must at least equal the length of the snake.

Although room-sized cages are needed by the giant pythons, small species such as the ball, Savu, and Children's python may be housed in plastic tubs with secure tops.

Types of Caging

Plastic Sweater Boxes

Plastic sweater boxes, with ventilation holes drilled or melted through the sides, are good for many species of smaller pythons. The smaller, shoebox-sized boxes can come in very handy if you suddenly hatch a clutch of eggs and have anywhere from 6–40 babies to deal with. When the babies are housed one to a box, you can monitor each baby's growth and feeding response. Choose clear plastic boxes over the translucent ones—those made of translucent plastic make observing your pet impossible.

You can fit many of these plastic boxes in a small amount of space, especially if you use a rack. A shoebox rack is very easy to build; it is essentially a bank of shelves with a heat tape set either in the front or along the back edge of the shelves. The heat tape, a flat strip designed to heat a glass terrarium from under-neath, is an economical and efficient way to provide a warmth gradient for each shoebox, and may be purchased from most pet stores.

Glass Terraria

Glass aquariums are for most of us the simple way out. In the 20-gallon or less size, they're relatively easy to move, easy to clean, and not very expensive. The screen tops which clip into place are sturdy enough to prevent the escape of the smaller pythons. The larger all-glass tanks which are specifically designed for use as terraria have tops with sliding screened panels. A tank which measures 4 × 2 × 2 feet is large enough for a six-to-eight-foot-long snake.

Cage height comes into play when you opt for an arboreal python, such as the green tree python. Arboreal snakes need tree branches, and the caging needs to accommodate the height. With a few adjustments, standard aquaria/terraria can be adapted.

Constructing a Stacked Tank

1. You'll need two tanks of the same dimensions, a hammer, newspapers, and heavy gloves. Safety glasses should be worn.

2. Put a pad of newspapers on a firm floor (cement or vinyl flooring), unfolded so that you can wrap up the broken glass.

3. Turn the tank-to-be-bottomless upside down and cover the bottom within an inch or so of the frame surrounding the bottom with duct tape or the two-inch wide wrapping tape you use for mailing. This will keep most of the glass stuck on the tape and make pick-up and disposal much easier. Turn the tank rightside up on the newspaper pad.

4. Add another pad of newspapers inside the tank, extending slightly up the sides of the tanks. You don't want stray bits of glass to fly upward and cut you.

5. Tap the bottom gently with a hammer until you hear it break, then tap along the perimeter of the tank.

6. Lift the newspaper to check your progress. When the glass has broken free, lift the tank and fold a couple of sheets of newspaper around the broken bottom and throw it away. Use the pliers to wiggle out the pieces near the perimeter of the tank.

7. Place the bottomless tank atop the second tank and add a strip of wide packing or duct tape across the back seam. Two shorter pieces of tape with folded-under pull-tabs can be added on the sides. When you place the stacked tanks in your snake room, put them about six inches from a wall. This will enable you to loosen the side tabs of tape and tilt the top tank back against the wall. This will make getting to the bottom of the lower tank for cleaning much easier.

8. Once the top tank has lost its bottom, it has lost much of its structural integrity and must be handled gently even when secured atop the other tank.

Be careful when you knock the bottom out of a tank.

On the side: Consider turning a standard tank onto its short side and gluing rubber feet (rubber stoppers work well) underneath. Add substrate and branches, clip a screen top onto the open side, and you've got a vertical format tank.

Stacking: If you remove the bottom from a standard 20-gallon tank, you can stack that tank atop a second tank. Secure the two together with two-inch wide package tape, add substrate, tree limbs, and a clip-on screen top, and you have a vertical tank large enough for a chondro python. Do not use a solid top; pythons (and chondros in particular) need the ventilation and air flow afforded by a screen top. Commercially made mesh tank toppers can be purchased, if you don't need to keep the entire cage warm.

Cages that can be co-joined are useful for the larger species; the cage's area can be increased as the snake grows.

Glass-Fronted Boxes

These wooden cages are an older style of snake caging but one that is particularly good for larger snakes from a security viewpoint. These cages are generally made of 5/8" plywood, with a sliding or hinged glass front, or a hinged top. The open side is secured by a hasp, and ventilation holes are drilled in the sides, back, and top. The light is suspended from the top.

Certainly this type of caging can easily be made up to a floor area of 4 × 8 feet, the size of a single sheet of plywood. For the larger pythons—those up to 10 feet—these cages work well. Consider lining the cage with a cabinet-quality mica for ease of cleaning.

TIP

Too Close for Comfort?

The plywood box type tends to be a little "close" unless special care is taken to add ventilation panels on the back, sides, and top. The dimensions of this type of cage, rather low and long, make it hard to set up any type of cage decoration or accessory. For the larger snakes, any type of cage decoration is temporary, because the weight and strength of these snakes simply move it, knock it down, or flatten it.

Commercial Caging

Commercially made or custom cages are molded plastic or plastic laminate over plywood. These cages are easy to clean and come in a wide variety of sizes, and their uniform

Commercially made plastic boxes and racks allow you to provide individualized housing for a lot of snakes in a fairly compact area.

appearance gives a neat appearance to a reptile collection.

For Advanced Keepers: The Room-Sized Cage

Large pythons, like reticulated and Burmese pythons over 10 feet long, need a great deal of space. Snakes this large are generally too heavy and strong to keep in other cage types. Many python keepers find it easiest to devote an entire room to a snake this large. Such a room will need a climbing surface placed along one wall—cement blocks which are covered with enough cement to provide a roughened climbing surface work well. You'll need to seal all surfaces with a durable, waterproof surface. The floor can be bare cement or you can add vinyl flooring. The installation of a central drain will facilitate cleaning with a hose. Plan for adequate ventilation, either through reinforced screened windows or a standard HVAC ductwork. If the idea of wafting the odor of your snake cage through your entire house bothers you, you can add a separate unit just for that room.

Other caging requirements: In addition to the temperature control afforded by the HVAC system, you'll need to add some heat/light lamps to provide a hot spot for your python. If you create a sturdy sunning shelf

Most pythons are terrestrial and don't require vertical caging, so low, long caging gives them sufficient floor area.

near the ceiling, you can aim the lights at that point. Be certain that the snake cannot get close enough to the light to burn or injure itself. Your snake will need incandescent lighting for heating; fluorescent lights don't produce enough heat, and the ceramic heat lamps by themselves won't provide any light.

The water bowl should be untippable and large enough for your snake to submerge itself, and remember the incredible amount of water that can be displaced by a large python. Allow enough freeboard between the level of the water and the top edge of the watering trough. You may choose

Although hobbyists are infatuated with aberrant colors, some designer green tree pythons seem to diminish the image normally perpetuated by this species.

to install a bathtub, complete with a water source and a drain, for your water container. Snakes often stool in their water dish (particularly just after it has been cleaned), and you'll need an easy way to drain, clean, and refill it.

Feeding a large python is easiest and safest if the snake is moved to a separate box for feeding. The snake then associates the box with food, instead of associating the entrance of people into its cage with food.

If this isn't an option, feeding a large python will take two people; one to throw in the pre-killed food, and a second to watch the python's reaction when it smells the food and detects the motion of its keeper in its cage. If you're going to change/clean the watering dish and feed your snake in the same day, clean the water bowl *before* you handle the food animals. Once that task is done, your entry into the cage

a second time—this time smelling of food—will be safer.

Substrate

What you use on the floor of the cage is partially determined by the size of caging you select. For the ultra-simple sweater boxes, the substrate can be mulch, paper towels, or newspaper. For cages larger than 6 × 12 inches, mulch or newspapers work better than paper towels.

Cypress or aspen mulch (or wood shavings) gives the best tradition for crawling. It is absorbent enough to absorb liquid from the snake's stools or from an overturned water dish, and the small snakes may burrow into it if it's deep enough. You can spot-clean simply by lifting out the debris. Every month or so, you simply throw out the old mulch and replace it with new. It looks attractive, and you can add a few plants simply by burying the pots up to their rim in the mulch. The only caution with shavings or mulch is to avoid any form of cedar—cedar is loaded with phenols which are deadly to all reptiles (and amphibians, for that matter). Pine shavings have also lapsed into disfavor because of their phenol content.

Paper towels are easy to replace when soiled, quickly absorb liquids, and make finding your snakes within the cage easy. If you add a second folded towel in one half of the cage, the snake may utilize the folded portion as a hiding area. The downside is that paper towels don't afford much purchase for crawling, and they are too lightweight and rumple too easily to use in any cages larger than shoebox-size. It is also difficult to make the cage look at all natural by adding plants or pieces of bark.

Newspapers are hard to beat for a substrate, especially for smaller pythons. It is very utilitarian and satisfactory for those who want a unadorned cage. When soiled, it is easily changed. It doesn't look particularly attractive, and the snakes will find crawling on it more difficult because it affords essentially no purchase. You may wish to start out with newspaper, but as time goes on, you probably will want to provide a more attractive environment for your snakes.

Indoor-outdoor carpeting is used by some keepers. Cut to the size of the cage, the carpet lies flat and does look attractive. It does tend to absorb fecal liquids. The difficulty lies in cleaning the carpet sections. Certainly you can shake off the dried debris, but the absorbed portion is going to smell. You can scrub the carpeting in a wash tub; a kitchen sink or bathtub should not be used, due to basic hygiene concerns.

Hide Boxes

When setting up your cages, you need to provide adequate hiding areas (called hide boxes or simply "hides") for your snakes. It is always best to provide more than one hide box, one near the cage's hot spot and one further away, at the cooler end of the cage. You can use cardboard boxes with an access hole cut, or commercially available plastic boxes.

For climbing pythons, buy a box that has a wide lip around the rim (like a dishpan), cut an access hole at the rim, and mount the box on the ceiling of the cage. Use heavy "L-pins" (obtainable at a hardware store) to form tracks and slide the rim of the box into the track. In this setting pythons will feel secure and will rest with their head out of the entry hole, surveying the cage below.

About Cage Humidity

Cage humidity can be an important consideration in successful maintenance. Pythons from humid areas, like the chondro pythons, have trouble shedding if the humidity in the cage is too low. Arid-land python species, like the Stimson's python, languish if kept under too-humid conditions.

One of the easiest ways to control humidity in your cages is by judicious sizing of the water dish. Certainly all pythons need to have clean drinking water at all times, but a smaller dish in cages of arid-land pythons will help keep the humidity level down. If there is a heat tape or heating pad under part of the cage, make sure the water bowl is at the far end for the arid-land species. For pythons from humid areas, a larger water bowl will help maintain optimum humidity levels.

HOW-TO: CLEAN THE CAGE WITHOUT GETTING BITTEN

Some pythons, like the retics, are always bad tempered, and you can pretty much know to be careful around them at all times. Other pythons can become aggressive when they feel like it, or when triggered by hunger, the smell of food, or (in the case of males) by the sight or smell of another male python during breeding season. Sometimes these moods occur when they are least expected and least wanted—like during cage cleaning.

Certainly the best way to clean a python's cage thoroughly and safely is to remove the python while you work. The python can be "hooked" and placed in a covered container (we use 40 to 60 gallon plastic trash cans) while the cage is cleaned, disinfected (don't use a phenol-based cleanser!), rinsed, and dried. The snake hook is again employed to remove the snake from the container and replace it in its cage. And then we all know what happens. The snake, disturbed and with its metabolism correspondingly raised, stools in the freshly cleaned cage and the whole procedure must happen again.

Sometimes cleaning a python's cage, no matter the size of the animal, can be simple and straightforward. This is especially so if the snake is resting in a hide box or is tightly coiled in a soaking tub. You merely cover the front of the box or the top of the tub and go about the business of cleaning. But there may be those times when the snake is actively watching you with a level of attention that is different than usual. If that is the case, and if it is possible to do so, delay the cleaning.

If it is not possible to delay, use a solid baffle of some type to contain the snake. Even then, if it is a big snake (meaning over eight feet long), be careful. Cleaning the cage of a snake larger than 10 feet should be considered a two-person job—one to clean after the other has contained the snake (most pythons will readily enter a hide box where they can be contained through the cleaning) or diverted its attention. Use care and respect whenever working with big snakes.

BASIC HUSBANDRY

Pythons, like other snakes, need specific care in order to flourish. Make certain that you have both sexes of your python species if you want to breed them.

Sexing

If the snakes are ones that you purchased as babies and raised, then they should have been sexed as soon as you received them, so any errors could be addressed with your supplier.

If you're not certain you have both sexes, there are three ways to find out.

"Popping"

Most hatchling pythons can be sexed by popping or manually everting the hemipenes. This is done just after hatching or within a few days of hatching, while the snake itself is still very pliable. Grasp the hatchling by the rear of the body, turn the snake over, and place your thumb on the underside of the tail, about half an inch behind the cloaca. Apply gentle but

The scrub python is also known as the amethystine python. Although rather slender, it may attain a length of more than 20 feet. This is a hatchling.

firm pressure, and roll your thumb all the way to the cloacal opening. If the hatchling is a male, the hemipenes should evert, appearing as short, red stubs. If no hemipenes appear, the snake is a female.

Probing

For older snakes, you'll need to probe the snake to determine the length of the hemipenes (males) or the musk glands (females). In this process, a lubricated shaft of the proper dimension (the probe) is inserted into the cloacal opening of the snake. The male's hemipenes are longer than the female's musk glades, and so the depth to which the probe can be inserted reveals the snake's sex.

To probe a snake, hold the tail of the snake in one hand and turn it upside-down. The probe (lubricated with K-Y Jelly or Vaseline) is inserted into the cloacal opening of the snake in the direction of the tail. The depth is meas-ured by counting the number of subcaudal scales. For the females, the probe can generally be inserted to the depth of 2-4 subcaudal scales. A probe inserted into a male snake, on the other hand, can be inserted the total length of the hemipenis, generally to a depth of 8-15 subcaudal scales.

Probing works on all pythons except for chondros and those types with short tails. For ball pythons and the blood pythons, the hemipenes and the musk gland are about the same length, and probing is inconclusive. (Sexing these pythons is very much an educated guess, based on general appearance and width of the tail. Baby chondros are sold unsexed.)

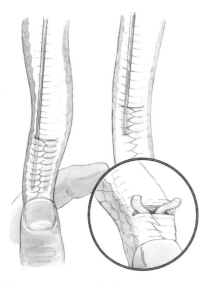

Probing is the most reliable way of sexing an adult snake (male left, female right). Hatchlings (in circle) may be manually sexed (a male with everted hemipenes is depicted), but this should be done by an experienced person (not recommended for tree boas and green tree pythons).

TIP

Warning

There are a couple of cautions to remember before you try manual eversion. Do not use this technique on a hatchling that is about to shed, because the skin can easily be torn at this time. Do not use this technique on hatchling green tree pythons, where it will cause tail kinking problems. Don't use this technique on snakes that are older than a few days, because the pressure you apply may cause permanent tail kinking and/or damage the hemipenes.

Appearance

It is also possible to sex your snakes by looking at the tail. Males usually have longer spurs than the females; these are located outside the cloaca and are very obvious. If the female does have spurs, they are very tiny. Another difference is that the male has a wider, longer tail than the female.

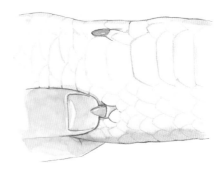

The pelvic spurs of a male boid are typically larger than those of a female.

Obviously, these comparison calls mean you need to have at least two snakes—and preferably of the opposite sex—to be able to see what "wider" means or what "longer spurs" look like.

Lighting

Lighting can be provided by either incandescent bulbs or fluorescent lighting. Most snakes do not seem to need full spectrum lighting; generations have been raised under ordinary lights.

The day/night cycle is important to regulate your python's circadian rhythm. Many snake keepers will reduce the winter cycle to eight or nine hours of light and allow the summer cycle to build up to 16 hours of light. The easiest way to keep your snakes on a natural light cycle is to alter the daily cycle by five minutes a day or 30 minutes a week to mimic seasonal changes.

There are some unanswered questions about how important day length is to the breeding cycle. Temperature seems to play a more important role. Those breeders who change their cycles are not sure if it helps, but assume that it may be useful—certainly it does not hurt anything. Breeders in the Pacific Northwest have been successful in breeding pythons without altering the usual 12-12 day-night split, and in Florida when the day/night cycles were altered to match the seasons.

Feeding

What to Feed

The majority of pythons kept in captivity are fed a rodent diet, meaning mice, rats, or (rarely) hamsters. Larger pythons, those over eight feet long, need or prefer larger prey.

Offer prekilled prey items—feeding live mice (or rats) to your python is asking for trouble. Every veterinarian has dealt with pet pythons with the gnawed-off tail tip, the pierced eye, the partially eaten vertebral column, and heard the owner wail, "I never thought a live mouse would hurt my snake!" Pythons do not need to kill their own prey, nor do they need to constrict their prey in order to feed.

Even if you put all humanitarian feelings for mice or rats aside and operate from a purely practical perspective, keeping food for your pythons on hand is easier if the food items can be stored in your freezer. You can buy frozen mice or rats at your local pet shop, or you can order them in quantities online.

Many pythons readily eat birds, which is easy to handle once you find a steady source of chickens, chicks, or even quail. Like other feeder animals, frozen chicks are available online in whatever quantity you need. The downside of feeding birds of any kind is that they frequently cause loose stools. This may create more mess than a snake owner is willing to put up with.

It is best to get all young pythons on a diet of mice; mice are far easier to obtain year-round than any other food item. But some hatchling pythons, especially *Anteresia*, may refuse pinkies. You can help persuade young pythons to eat mice or pinkies by scenting that food item with a lizard.

One way is to keep a lizard tail in your freezer and to rub the head of the pinkie or mouse with it. You can also create a scenting gruel for dipping the head of warm-blooded prey items by chopping up a skink tail and boiling it in a cup of water. You can freeze the gruel in a mini-ice cube tray, and then empty the cubes into a plastic bag kept in your

Some anthill pythons may be reluctant to accept small mice as prey, holding out instead for an offering of geckos.

freezer. Thaw a cube when you need to scent food. A commercial lizard-scenting liquid is available, but we have not tried it.

How Often to Feed

Pythons, like other snakes, don't require much food (rattlesnakes in the wild may eat only twice a year). Feed your adult python every two to six weeks, hatchling every week. During breeding season, both males and females may go off-feed, and gravid females may stop feeding. Pythons may also go off-feed during the cooler winter months.

How to Feed

Thawing frozen food items is easy and takes surprisingly little time. We thaw them in warm water (it takes about 20 minutes, changing the water for warmer water at mid-point) and blot them dry. It is important that the food item be totally thawed before offering it to your snake. Do not use a microwave to thaw food items— it makes the food item soggy and creates hot spots which are deadly for your snake. Occasionally the food item will explode in the microwave, which is exceedingly hard to explain and almost impossible to totally remove. Use

Because some ball pythons may be difficult to induce to eat, it is always a good idea to ascertain that the one you choose is feeding readily.

a long pair of tongs to offer a mouse or rat to each of the smaller pythons. Generally it only takes a feeding or two for the snakes to catch on to the process and to eagerly accept the food items. Occasionally we need to tease the snake by gently tapping it on the nose with the food item, and slightly withdrawing it.

Feeding the larger pythons takes a little more care. You'll need to supply a feeding box—a ventilated and latchable or securable box (or garbage can). The snake is hooked and placed in the feeding box and the top closed. The thawed food items are added, and the top secured

again. If using a separate food box is not an option for a larger snake, feeding the snake will take two people, one to watch the snake and intervene if needed, and the second to toss the food item into the cage.

If the larger python does not begin to feed within a few minutes, open the food box and use a baffle between you and the snake while you remove the food. The snake is returned to its cage, and you can repeat the process in two weeks. For pythons three feet or longer that are fed in their own cage, employ a baffle to shield yourself while you remove any uneaten food.

With exotic animals like pythons, it is very important to locate a good veterinarian who has had experience with reptiles before your run into a problem.

Quarantine Procedures

The most important thing you can do to protect the health of your python collection is to quarantine incoming animals for a month, in a room apart from the room where your collection is kept. This isolation is very important, because some snake diseases are both highly infectious and fatal.

When a new snake arrives, remove it from the bag and examine the snake closely. Make certain it is the sex you ordered. Look for any wounds and check the snake's mouth to make sure it is pink-white and free from any cheesy areas of debris. Look closely for snake mites. Always examine the bag that held the snake, since the little black mites will show up well against the white cloth. This bag should be washed and dried (preferably in an electric or

A hatchling chondro, in the red phase.

gas dryer—the heat helps kill any mites) before being used for any other snakes.

Quarantine Your Snake

1. Place your snake in a clean cage with fresh water and a hide box. Provide a hot spot, and keep the rest of the cage from 80–87°F (27–30°C) during the day and 75–85°F (24–29°C) at night.

2. Wait at least 24 hours before offering pre-killed food.

3. During the next two or three weeks, watch for any signs of mites. A mite infestation may be indicated by the snake soaking in its water bowl for protracted periods, the snake twitching its skin nervously, or by swollen areas under the snake's belly scutes. The mites themselves are visible to your naked eye, especially near the snake's eyes.

4. Watch your snake as it crawls. Does it have any difficulty in crawling? Does it flick its

Inspect both your snake and the bag it came in for evidence of mites

the cloacal area while you massage the ventral surface of the snake towards the vent. Your veterinarian can assist with this procedure if you need help.

6. After a month's time, if your snake has eaten at least once, has normal looking stools, does not look thin, and shows absolutely no sign of mites, you can incorporate the snake into your collection.

Before You Buy Your Python

If you keep animals for any length of time, you'll encounter some kind of medical problems. You will need a veterinarian who will listen to you, ask you about your snake's environmental requirements, and then explain how those conditions might relate to the medical problem in question.

Finding a Veterinarian

The first place to start is your telephone book. Look under "Veterinarians" in the yellow pages; some veterinarians advertise their specialties with a display ad. Go online and type in "American Association of Reptile Veterinarians" to find one in your area. Call your local pet store, and ask which veterinarian takes care of their reptiles. Ask other reptile keepers in your area for the names of veterinarians they have used.

Once you've narrowed your search (and you may have only one or two to choose from), call the practice and ask about the veterinarian's experience. When there are a couple of veteri-

tongue as it crawls? (See the section on inclusion body disease if your snake has trouble crawling, or if it contorts its neck or seems to stare into space, and be forewarned: these are serious symptoms.)

5. Examine your snake's stools. A healthy snake has stools which are half solid and half liquid, half dark and half white. Take a sample stool to your veterinarian to check for parasites. If your newly arrived snake has not fed, the easiest way to get a stool specimen is to give the snake a bath in tepid water. If this does not work, it may be possible to obtain enough fecal material for an exam by gently manipulating

Although usually smaller, spotted pythons may attain 4 feet in length.

narians in a single practice, make sure that the one you want is scheduled to work the day of your appointment.

Some people try to avoid veterinarians because of the cost involved, but we feel this is very short-sighted. As many years as we have been keeping reptiles, we have regularly relied upon (and welcomed) the help and expertise of our veterinarians.

The Warm Cage

If you have a medical problem with one of your snakes, you need to be able to isolate this snake in a cage where the temperature can be elevated. Studies have shown that sick or injured snakes will deliberately seek out higher temperature and that this seems to help them recover. Where you are dealing with a respiratory problem, with an injury, or with mouth rot, you should always be prepared to provide a "warm cage."

The most effective temperature seems to be a constant 90°F both day and night. This should be maintained for a week or 10 days, or as long as your snake is on medication. Be certain that plenty of clean drinking water is available.

When your snake has a problem such as an abscess, mouth rot, or a respiratory issue, using

Obstruction of the lachrymal ducts may cause a fluid buildup between the eye and the eyecap. This will require veterinary intervention.

a warm cage can speed recovery even before medication is begun. Your veterinarian may want to start a course of antibiotics.

Shedding

Snake shedding is one of the most useful indicators of what is going on with your captive python. It gives you distinct clues about reproductive cycles, parasite infestations, illness, and general health. There are some very specific times in your python's life that sheds will occur and this can provide you with some useful information if you can interpret it correctly.

The first time a snake sheds is a few days after hatching. Following this, the sheds should occur fairly regularly throughout your snake's growth to adulthood.

Once adulthood has been reached, the sheds take on more significance. Female reproductive sheds occur after a cooling period, just prior to ovulation. The snake will shed again in several weeks (the pre-egg-laying shed), and once more after laying the eggs (the post-egg-laying shed). These are all useful indicators that will be discussed in the breeding section.

Aside from the predictable sheds mentioned above, your python should have a fairly uniform rate of shedding under normal, non-breeding circumstances. Sheds outside the normal periodicity should always be evaluated for possible causes. If snake mites get into your collection and infest a snake, the snake's response is to initiate a shed. Injuries to the skin, such as burns, will also initiate more frequent sheds during the healing process.

Other health problems can stimulate frequent sheds. If you have a snake that is shedding frequently and doesn't look quite right to you,

take it to your veterinarian for a general examination. It would also be wise to bring a stool specimen with you for this examination.

Parasites

Mites and Ticks

Ticks are blood-sucking, teardrop-shaped arachnids that are common on wild-caught animals, but the animal you receive should be tick-free. That being said, at one time or another, be prepared to find a tick or two on your python, usually attached near the eyes or head. They are easy to see, because they measure from 1/8-1/4" across and are dark brown or gray in color. They aren't particularly attractive, but in lower numbers they don't generally represent a serious health hazard. Researchers are still undecided whether ticks are a vector in inclusion body disease, so prompt removal of these parasites is still a good idea.

When you find a tick on your snake, use a pair of tweezers to grasp the parasite by its head (not the body), and with a steady but firm pressure, pull it off the snake. Don't pull it sharply, because you want to remove the entire creature. After you remove the tick, you can swab the bite site with a bit of alcohol or a cotton ball moistened with soapy water. Check your python in a week or so for any ticks you may have missed the first time, and remove them.

Mites are more of a problem than ticks, because they are smaller, harder to eradicate, and have been implicated in the spread of some serious snake diseases. The blood loss from a heavy infestation can weaken and kill a snake.

Mite infestations can be detected partly by looking at the snake and partly by the snake's

Puffy skin around the eyes and a dusty appearance such as shown on this rough-scaled python may indicate a mite infestation.

behavior. The snake's skin may have an opaque or pale look to it. A snake with mites is restless and will sometimes rub against the sides of its cage to try to dislodge the little burrowing arachnids. The snake will soak in its water dish to try to drown the mites. The snake may go into a shed to try to get rid of the mites, but none of these actions will work in the confines of a cage unless you lend a hand. You need to not only get the mites off the snakes—which is comparatively easy—but you have to eliminate the mites from all the nooks and crannies in the cage. Do not put off treatment if you see mites on just one snake. Mites can spread rapidly through an entire collection.

Clean the cage: Cages that have mites in them should be taken out of your snake room, stripped of all decorations, thoroughly cleaned (use a dilute bleach solution and a scrub brush, at the very least) and let dry. Spray the cage with a reptile mite killer.

Replace cage accessories with new accessories that you are certain are mite-free. We once tried to eradicate mites from a section of cholla cactus skeleton that we particularly liked. We dunked it in boiling water, left it in our freezer for a week, then slow-roasted it in the oven at 250 degrees. Once it cooled, we put it back in the cage. A week later we noticed the mites were back. At that point we figured that the cage had not been properly cleaned, so we went to work again and cleaned the cage, repeated our cleaning of the cholla, and treated the cage inhabitants once again. The problem did not reoccur.

Mites on your snake: Most pet shops carry specific products made to kill mites on reptiles, or you can find them online. Your veterinarian can help with a prescription containing Ivermectin.

Soaking: If you are keeping some of the smaller pythons and don't want to use insecti-

Once known as the Irian Jaya carpet python, this snake is now called the Papuan carpet python and is scientifically designated as **Morelia spilota harrisoni.**

cides on your snake, place the snake in a tepid container of water for a couple of hours to drown the majority of the mites. We have used a five-gallon bucket, with holes poked through the lid, or plastic aquarium with a plastic snap-on lid. After soaking (the snake will move around in the container, both below and above the water during this time), remove the snake, dry it and give it a light coating of cooking oil or mineral oil. Pay particular attention to the area around the eyes and under the chin, both places that mites like to hide in. The oil will help suffocate the mites, and after an hour or two you can wipe your snake down and return it to its cage, which you have cleaned, sprayed, and dried in the interim.

You'll need to repeat this soaking at weekly intervals for about a month.

Prevention is easier than eradication with mite infestations. The best solution is to examine any new snake very carefully and to deal with any mite problem before the snake is added to your collection.

Internal Parasites

Symptoms: If your python is thin and not gaining weight or has loose, foul-smelling stools, the snake should be tested for internal parasites. This is particularly true if your python was wild-caught. Keep in mind that not all internal parasites must be eliminated; we don't know yet what role some of them may play in digestion. It's when the balance of internal parasites gets altered that you need to intervene.

Diagnosis: Take a fresh stool specimen to your veterinarian to find out what parasites are involved. Experience has shown us that the sudden killing of several types of parasites at once, using a broad-spectrum parasiticide, can cause more problems than the parasites themselves. It is probably wise to follow a conservative course, treating for one type of parasite at a time and then giving a rest period before treating for another.

Respiratory Problems

Respiratory problems are often bacterial in origin and in the early stages can be diagnosed simply by an excess of mucus in the snake's mouth. The bacteria destroy the lining of the lung and trachea, and it is the liquid contents from these cells that you are seeing. Less severe cases can be noticed when the snake rubs its face against the glass front of its enclosure and leaves a wet smear, or when the snake holds its mouth slightly ajar. In severe cases, the snake may hold its head elevated and a pocket of mucus will form, causing a bulge in the throat. A gurgling or raspy sound will be made when the snake tries to breathe. Your snake is in trouble.

Causes: Respiratory problems are usually triggered by exposure to a cage that is too cold (pythons cannot take temperatures less than 65°F), stress, or possibly a severe mite infestation. Occasionally the stress of reproduction can trigger this problem.

Treatments: If the problem appears to be severe, don't wait—take your snake to your veterinarian. A hot water bottle packed with your snake will help maintain a safe warmth if the outside temperature is below 70°F (21°C).

If the problem is not acute, you can begin treatment on your own. The first step is to put the snake in its own cage and to elevate the cage

temperature. This may enable your snake to fight off the infection. If the snake doesn't look better in a day's time, take it to your veterinarian.

Regurgitation

There are both environmental and internal causes of regurgitation, and sometimes the two can play off each other. The environmental causes are straightforward, like feeding too much at a time, or letting the cage cool too much after feeding. Keeping the cage too warm is another cause.

Regurgitation can also be caused by a bloom of intestinal flora. Normally present intestinal flora can, under stressful conditions, increase to pathogenic numbers. Wild-caught animals undergo a lot of stress in getting from their home to yours. The conditions of capture may be difficult; the python is generally noosed and then bagged. After several days—or even a week

═══ TIP ═══

Regurgitation Syndrome

When the cause cannot be identified and you've been unsuccessful in persuading your snake to keep a meal down and digesting it, the diagnosis may be regurgitation syndrome, and *then* you will be cautioned to keep your snake away from all of your other snakes. Snakes with regurgitation syndrome usually die a lingering death of starvation and starvation-related diseases. It is thought to be communicable to other snakes.

or two—the snake is dumped from the bag into a large container (metal cattle troughs with screened lids are typical) with other snakes. Temperature maintenance is uncertain at best, and water may or may not be offered. After a few more weeks, the snake is re-bagged and shipped to the U.S. to a wholesaler, or perhaps directly to you. A snake with normal gut flora and feeding response would be a rarity under these conditions. A captive-born python can experience this same sort of problem when stressed by shipping, or by changes in its environment too subtle for its keeper to pick up on.

What to do: Whether wild-caught or captive-hatched, the beginning treatment is the same. Isolate the snake in a warm, quiet cage for a week or so and offer smaller meals, both

in size and number. If the problem continues, take the python and a stool specimen to your veterinarian.

Mouth Rot

Mouth rot is a catch-all term for any infectious disease of the mouth. A more technical term is infectious stomatitus, which lets you know that the problem is infectious and can be transmitted to other snakes. The "stomatitus" portion literally means inflammation of the mouth or stoma. There may be several different causes.

Symptoms: You may first realize there is a problem when you see that your snake cannot close its mouth.

Diagnosis: When you hold the snake and gently open its mouth (use both hands for this—use the fingers of one hand to catch the throat skin and pull it down, while holding the upper jaw with the thumb and forefinger of the other hand), you may be able to see lines of cheesy-looking material next to the teeth in either the upper or lower jaw. The lining of the mouth may be red and discolored. Certainly this problem needs to be treated.

Treatment: Try lifting out the cheesy material, using a cotton swab dipped in water or dipped in a very dilute saline solution. Apply Polysporin ointment to the affected areas with a cotton swab (Polysporin ointment and Polysporin cream can be purchased at your drugstore without a prescription; the ointment is oil-based and tends to cling better than the cream). Elevate the cage temperature for a

Both pattern and coloration are aberrant on this pretty "fancy" ball python.

Some scrub pythons, like this one, bear dark markings, but many are of rather uniform coloration.

week to 10 days. Check and treat the mouth daily until the signs are gone.

Getting help: If the cheesy material does not come away cleanly, or if the mouth is red, discolored, and bleeding, you need a veterinarian's assistance with this problem. Again, use a warm cage during treatment with any prescribed medications.

Viral and Retroviral Problems

As with humans, there is no effective python treatment for viral or retroviral problems. Retroviruses are very minute, just-larger-than-virus-sized bits of pathogenic DNA, and they are so new to reptile medicine as to be successfully identified only at necropsy. Both viral and retroviral infections are diagnosed partially by symptoms and partly by the lack of response to any treatment.

Inclusion body disease is a fatal disease characterized by regurgitation, followed by central nervous system (CNS) disorders (including head tremors and the inability of the snake to right itself if turned over). The snake also loses the inability to focus its eyes and exhibits a characteristic upward staring behavior called star-gazing.

The disease is thought to be caused by a retrovirus, and is probably transmitted from snake to snake by mites. The name, inclusion body disease (IBD), was coined when captive snakes began to display what are now classic CNS problems and subsequently died, and the only out-of-the-ordinary finding was scattered dark areas or inclusion bodies inside body cells.

IBD can spread though your entire collection and there is no treatment and no cure. The only effective control is through the quarantine of incoming animals and the immediate humane killing and sanitary disposal of the remains.

BREEDING

Even if breeding is not one of your goals, learning about the process will help you better understand your snake's behavior.

For many python keepers, getting their pythons to reproduce is a test of their husbandry skills. In the northern hemisphere, breeding season coincides with the shortest days of the year, December to April. A few species breed in the fall, but the majority of pythons in our hemisphere breed during the winter.

Age

Sexual maturity appears to be a function of size rather than age, and with some exception most pythons can reproduce when two-thirds to three-quarters grown. For ball pythons, for instance, males can successfully breed at about two feet in length, whereas the females rarely breed before reaching three feet in length.

Young breeders often produce smaller clutches of eggs than older, more mature animals. The incidence of reproductive failure is much higher for younger snakes, and most

Green tree pythons may simply drop their eggs if no suitable egg box is provided.

breeders prefer not to "push" their female snakes in this fashion.

Animals not in the peak of health may yield infertile or retained eggs. The female especially needs to have good fat reserves and good body weight to produce a viable clutch of eggs. She will not feed from the time she becomes gravid until she lays her eggs. If she incubates

TIP

Plan in Advance

Before you place the animals together, give some thought to what you will do if your snakes breed successfully. You'll need to plan on how you will house, feed, monitor, and otherwise deal with the young. (Selling/giving away from 10-60 hatchlings is not as easy or as quick as you might think. Chain pet stores do not obtain animals locally—even if they are free.)

Albinism in the reticulated python has been known for decades. This hatchling was offered for sale at a captive breeder's expo.

her eggs, her non-feeding will continue until the eggs hatch. It will take time to put weight back on a female after deposition or incubation. Males will stop feeding during the breeding season, and so they also need to begin the season at good weight.

Cycling to Induce Breeding

Temperature Cycles

Temperature fluctuations seem to be the most important cue in inducing python breeding.

Cool the evenings: Most breeders will cycle their pythons at the beginning of the breeding season by dropping the evening temperature to around 70°F for a period of six to eight hours, and then raising the daytime temperature back to normal levels. This is done for about a month prior to introducing the sexes to each other, and for about a month afterward. At the end of this time, temperatures should be returned to their normal day and night levels. Most breeders begin this cooling process in November and early December.

Copulation

Adding the male: Once you've cycled your pythons to ready them for breeding, you can introduce the male into the female's cage. Courtship may begin almost immediately, with the male following the female around the cage and then crawling over her. Both snakes will be flicking their tongues as they take in what must be a powerful series of pheromone scents.

Sperm viability: Sometimes copulation will occur at night and may not be observed, but when you do see a copulation, it usually lasts for an hour or so.

Using two males: You can stimulate copulation in your snakes by using two males, but sequentially. Males placed together at this time of the year are apt to fiercely bite each other and anything else within reach. The safe way to use two males is to place one male in the female's cage, let him crawl around for a few minutes, and then remove him. Immediately introduce another male into the female's cage, while the scent of the first male is still present.

Gravid Females

Is she? There are a number of indicators which indicate that a female is gravid. Within 10 days of copulation you may notice "mid-body bulge" in your female. This will appear as a distinct and noticeable swelling, as though a meal has just been eaten, but will disappear within 24 to 48 hours. Radiographs have shown that these are the ova changing position in the female's body, moving forward from the ovaries to the oviducts, where they will be fertilized by the waiting sperm.

As the eggs develop, some of the female's fat reserves will be used up and the back third of her body will become swollen, developing a pear-shaped appearance. At this stage, many females will go off feed as the body becomes filled with enlarging eggs. Regular basking behavior will usually be observed, often with the female turning the back half of her body upside down as she basks.

The hot-spot: It is extremely important to provide a basking area for the female during the period she is carrying eggs. Gravid females will regularly bask at a heat source and will provide

The albino Burmese python was the first aberrant color of what now seems a never-ending succession of color mutations.

some interesting behavior for you to observe as they thermoregulate their bodies, moving toward and then away from the heat source.

Shedding before laying: Most females will undergo a pre-laying shed, which occurs about a month prior to egg laying. This shedding is a useful tool in letting you know when to expect—and to prepare for—egg laying.

Nesting Sites

Provide the site: It is always a good idea to provide some kind of shelter supplied with moistened sphagnum moss as a nest site for your

tip of her nose showing. Do not expect her to be friendly at this time. Check her daily, especially at the one-month-after-her-last-shed date approaches. You'll need to decide if you'd like to incubate the eggs, or if you'd like the female to do the incubation—if she will. Once she has laid her eggs, the next step is up to you.

Laying the Eggs

Once the female has begun to lay her eggs, do not disturb her until she has completed the process. For most pythons, this will take about six to 10 hours. When she is done, you have just a few hours to remove them for incubation before they begin to stick together in a more or less coherent mass.

Taking the Eggs Away

To remove the eggs: For smaller species, you can wear a pair of leather gloves to protect your hands as you uncoil the female from around her eggs, pick the eggs up, and nestle them singly in the incubation sphagnum or vermiculite. Use a pencil to mark the upper side of the eggs, so you can keep this side up.

For larger species such as the Burmese or reticulated pythons, the simplest way to remove the eggs is to throw a blanket completely over the snake. Then reach in under the front edge of the blanket, lift the coils, and push them backwards over and beyond the eggs. Pick up the eggs, mark the top side with a penciled "x" and put them in the incubator. As you handle each egg, look for any that are smaller than the rest, yellowish, or misshapen. These are infertile and should be discarded.

gravid female. There have been some observations that gravid female pythons without egg deposition sites actually will retain the eggs, or, as in the case of the green tree python, simply let the eggs fall to the cage bottom.

With smaller species, a plastic box with an entry hole will suffice. With the really giant pythons it may not be feasible to build a covered box, but you can provide a large deep tray of moistened medium, or simply pile the dampened sphagnum on the floor of the cage. The female snake will generally move the sphagnum aside to lay her eggs, but you can nestle the sphagnum around her to provide humidity for the eggs.

Place the site: Where you place the egg deposition box inside your cage depends on the kind of python. With arboreal species such as the green tree python, the box should be hung on the wall of the cage; gravid chondros do not descend to the cage floor for egg deposition.

Terrestrial species need a box on the bottom of the cage.

Once you've placed the egg deposition box within the cage, the gravid female should begin exploring it, crawling into it and out again, and smelling it thoroughly with her tongue. As her due date approaches, she will spend more and more time within the box, often with just the

Caution

If a gravid female sheds, and if after four weeks she hasn't laid her eggs, consult with your veterinarian. The eggs may need to be surgically excised, and unfortunately, these eggs will not hatch.

If the eggs have dried into one contiguous pile, try to gently separate them. If they stick together too firmly to take apart, remove the pile intact and place the eggs into the incubator. As they near their hatching date, the eggs tend to become less adhesive.

Taking the eggs singlehandedly is a bit ticklish, because the female tends to coil around, on top of, and in-between the eggs on the edge of the clutch. If she shifts suddenly in response to your hands, she may crush some of her eggs, and the eggs may shift from their original "this-side-up" position. If both of your hands are busy trying to pin the female and remove eggs at the same time, your face is left unprotected and uncomfortably close to the female.

Retained Eggs

Once the female has laid her eggs, check to make sure she hasn't retained any. These generally appear as egg-sized lumps in the lower half of the body. You can sometimes feel them by gently running her body through your hand.

If you discover retained eggs, wait a few weeks to see if she will pass the eggs on her own. Retained eggs are rarely viable, and if fully shelled, cannot be re-absorbed by the female. Your veterinarian may use an injection of Oxytocin, a hormone that stimulates egg laying, or opt for surgical intervention.

The rare Angola python looks quite like a negative image of a normal-colored ball python.

A Chondro by Any Other Name Is Still a . . . Green Tree Python

For some reason, hobbyists have kept using the one-time generic name of *Chondropython* when discussing the spectacular and increasingly popular green tree python.

Although it has a huge natural range—on New Guinea and its surrounding islands, as well as the Cape York Peninsula of Australia—there is only one species of the green tree python, *Morelia viridis*. Despite this—or perhaps because of it—the term "locale specific" is important when discussing chondros. When the discussion becomes serious, expect to hear locale names such as Jayapura, Aru, Biak, Wamena, Manakwari, Sarong, and Merauke. Some of these locales are islands, while other are peninsulas, seaports, or mountain valleys.

Despite the best efforts of chondro breeders, chondros have retained their characteristic (but variable) all-green, blue-on-green, or yellow-on-green appearance.

Soon after the beginning of this century, a few pale-to-bright yellow chondros arrived at dealers in the United States. They were immediately dubbed Canary chondros, a name that has now become synonymous with the green tree pythons from Kofiau Island. Not all Kofiau chondros were yellow—a few were a light lime green. But even these were beautiful.

Most of those from the original shipments have been placed in breeding programs, and many of these have begun reproducing. The few reports available indicate most of the offspring have retained the yellow coloration.

New color morphs such as this melanistic ball python are the goal of many breeders.

Ball pythons with a piebald (partially unpigmented) pattern are in great demand by advanced hobbyists.

Brooding Behavior

After egg laying, it is important to get the female to begin feeding again. Sometimes the female will still exhibit brooding behavior, remaining coiled in her egg deposition box and striking at any interloper, even though the eggs have been removed. Brooding females (or females that think they are brooding) do not feed, so you need to change this behavior. At the very least, remove the egg-laying box. Better still is to move the female to another cage. Provide her with a hiding area but not, of course, a brooding box. If you pass by the cage and see the female has resumed her brooding position, remove her from the cage and handle her for a few minutes. Carry her around your home or simply support her body in your arms for a while, or even place her in a clean muslin snakebag for an hour or so.

Usually a few days of special attention as described here will stop the brooding behavior.

Watch her carefully during this time and treat her immediately at the first sign of illness.

Genetics

With the wide variety of aberrant colors and patterns now available in captive-bred pythons, it is useful to understand a bit about how to breed for some of these traits. It is sometimes possible to combine different traits with one another, such as mixing color and pattern defects together. This enables you to create a new pattern or color variation, which is why there are over 50 different color morphs or patterns in ball pythons. Some people will occasionally try to create a new appearing snake by hybridizing two closely related species, but this is not recommended. These "mutts" have appeared on the market, but have been avoided by the majority of collectors simply because these snakes are a dead end.

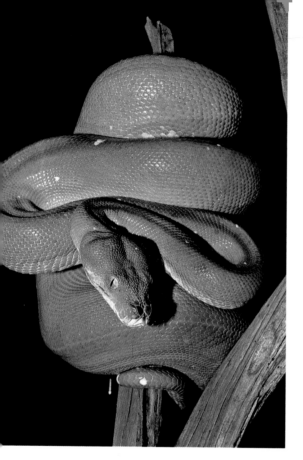

yellow), and iridiophores (which contain reflective crystals which result in khaki, blue, green, and red hues). Each type of color cell is in a specific layer within the skin.

Each color is determined by two genes, one dominant and the other recessive. Each snake carries two genes for each color or pattern. A snake with normal coloration has at least one dominant gene for normal coloration. If the second gene is for normal coloration, the snake can only pass on dominant genes for normal coloration.

But if a snake has one dominant gene for normal coloration and a recessive gene for albinism ("heterozygous" for albinism), breeding that snake with an albino (two recessive genes for albinism or "homozygous" for albinism) results in a split litter. Half of the young will appear normal, but bear one gene for normal coloration (the dominant gene) and the second gene for albinism (the recessive gene). These are heterozygous for albinism. The other half of the litter, the albinos, will have two recessive genes for albinism, and will be homozygous for albinism.

When you're dealing with four pigments, color variations and permutations seem pretty infinite. You can have a "red" albino, missing the black and yellow pigment; a "black" albino, missing the red and yellow pigment; a "white" albino, missing red, black, and yellow pigments, or a "yellow" albino, missing the red and black pigments.

There is no way to look at a snake of normal coloration and determine if it is heterozygous or homozygous; you have to know what the parents were.

When you combine two unrelated recessive genes such as coloration (we'll use albinism as

When you see a pattern or color variation in a snake, your first question is, "Is this genetic?" Many color and pattern variations are genetic, but some variations such as striping can also be caused by external factors during incubation, such as low incubation temperature.

The only way to know for sure is to breed for the trait you are interested in. This may take two generations to appear if the trait you are seeking is recessive.

Working with Color

In reptiles, colors in the skin are produced by three types of pigment cells, called melanophores (for brown and black), xanthophores (for red and

The green tree pythons from Kofiau Island may be a light lime green but are often bright yellow. They have been dubbed Canary chondros by hobbyists.

an example) and striping, the computations get a bit more complicated, but are still workable. The first clutch from this cross will be all normal babies, but double heterozygous, meaning carrying both recessive genes which are masked by the dominant gene. If you raise these babies and breed a pair of them to each other, you'll get a mixed bag in terms of appearance and genetics. The young of this cross will be three albino/normal patterned babies, three striped babies, nine normal color/normal patterned, three normal color/striped, and one albino-striped baby . . . the one you were trying to create. Once you get this first striped albino you can breed it in the same way as your original albino, to create a new line of snakes.

Those other babies in the litter can be sold. Pythons bearing recessive genes for desired colors or patterns are generally valued more than the normally colored, normally patterned babies.

When trying to reproduce new colors or patterns, it is sometimes necessary to inbreed brother to sister or mother to son. This first generation inbreeding is usually not harmful, but inbreeding should not be carried beyond this point. You should always keep a written record of your bloodlines and make every effort to breed unrelated snakes.

What Happens If I Breed for Some Unusual Mixes?

Breeding for special colors and patterns is still in its infancy, with a great deal of time, effort, and money being expended simply to discover the parameters of what breeds true and what doesn't. If a trait is thought to be recessive, at best the breeder needs to breed and raise to reproductive age three generations of snakes before a possible variant can be considered predictable.

INCUBATION

For anyone attempting to breed pythons, an incubator is a crucial piece of equipment.

Even if you choose to let the female incubate her eggs, an incubator "on standby" gives you the option of taking over the incubation process if something goes wrong. You can buy or make an incubator.

Commercial incubators range in price from about $60 for a simple box-design model to $4,000 for a sophisticated unit that will monitor heat, humidity, and carbon dioxide levels. Look in reptile trade magazines or online for suppliers.

These are a few of the components involved with any incubator:

1. It has to be large enough to hold all the eggs of your female.

2. Higher-cost incubators have a fan to circulate the air in the incubator and so keep the humidity and temperatures even. If you're dealing with the smaller species of python, with fewer and smaller eggs, the lack of a fan

Normal phase of the coastal carpet python.

is not as critical. But if you're breeding a large python (like the reticulated), the 60+ eggs produced take up a goodly amount of space. You'll need a larger incubator. A continuously operating fan does help keep moisture and heat levels evenly distributed.

3. The temperature needs to be controlled by two thermostats, wired in line with each other. If one fails, the second one can take over. For a homemade incubator, the wafer thermostats commonly used cost about $10 each, so the outlay for this type of security is modest.

4. A heat source. Commercial units may use a shielded heating coil. Home-made incubators utilize a heat tape. These, available from gardening or hardware stores, come in different wattages. We have found that a tape that uses 250–300 watts is large enough for an incubator about four feet square.

5. A ventilated shelving system. Shelves in the incubator should be made of screen or wire to permit easy flow air throughout the unit.

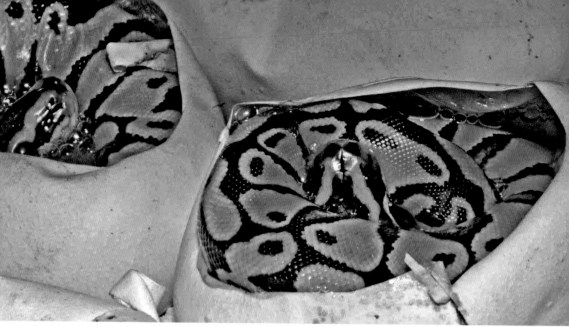

To display the babies to passersby at a herp expo, the top was removed from the eggs of these two ready-to-hatch fancy ball pythons.

Letting the Female Incubate Her Eggs

You certainly can let the female incubate her own eggs, particularly if caging temperatures are warm enough. Only a couple of species utilize quivering to generate heat for the eggs, so offer the option of access to additional heat. If the incubation site isn't warm enough, the female can leave the eggs to warm up and return. Ideally, for the female to successfully incubate her eggs, she and/or the eggs need temps from 86–90°F (ball pythons incubate their eggs in burrows that stay at near 95°F, with a humidity just over 80%). Let the female's behavior guide you here—if she leaves her eggs and stays away from them, the cage may be too warm, and the eggs will dry out.

Some female pythons will feed during the maternal incubation period, although most of them fast. The female will drink water during incubation, either by leaving the eggs and seeking out her water dish, or by drinking from her coils if misted.

The egg deposition box, with its layer of damp sphagnum, will help maintain the proper level of humidity, but you'll need to monitor the dampness of the sphagnum during the incubation period. If the female enters her drinking pool and then returns immediately to coil around her eggs, check the moisture level of the incubating medium. The female may be trying to remoisten her eggs by carrying moisture on her body surface. If needed, use a water spritzer to add moisture to the eggs.

Use remote digital thermometers and hydrometers to keep tabs on moisture and temperature levels. Disturb your incubating female as little as possible.

Artificial Incubation

Get ready: When your female shows signs of being gravid, get your incubator ready. Turn it on and let it warm up, to 88–90°F. Prepare a series of egg "storage" boxes with incubation medium and store them in the incubator.

The boxes used to house the eggs during incubation can be appropriately sized plastic boxes with ventilation holes and a solid lid. Incubation material can be moistened Perlite, sphagnum, peat moss, or vermiculite (to dampen, simply add water, stir to mix, then remove handfuls and squeeze until you can't squeeze any more water out. The medium should be damp enough to barely hold its shape when squeezed).

To remove the eggs of the smaller species of pythons, put on leather gloves to protect your hands as you gently uncoil the female from around her eggs. With larger species such as the Burmese, the simplest way to remove the eggs is to drape a blanket completely over the snake. Reach up under the front edge of the blanket, lift up the coils, and push them up and over the top of the eggs. Reach around both sides of the eggs and pull them toward you until they are free of the female's coils. The female snake will rarely bite during this process, unless mean to begin with. She may push at you or butt you with her coils, and this can be quite startling. Once you have removed the eggs, discard any that are small or misshapen. If they are caught in the middle of the clutch don't be afraid to gently pull the eggs away until you can loosen and discard the bad eggs. If you are unsure if some eggs are bad, incubate them. Your nose will tell you in about ten days if the egg is fertile or not.

Mark each egg with a penciled "x" to indicate the top side. Place them in the incubator, marked side up, and check the temperature daily. Add water to the incubating medium around the eggs as needed. The preferred humidity is 85–100%.

Determining Fertility

How do you know if the eggs are fertile? By the end of the first week, those eggs which are not fertile will turn yellow, harden, and begin to collapse. Those that are fertile will remain white and turgid to the touch. Infertile eggs may mold, but this is seldom transferred to healthy eggs.

During the first 6–8 weeks of incubation the eggs should gradually swell as they develop. If the eggs begin to indent, they are not getting enough moisture. Check the humidity level.

In the final week of incubation, most eggs will begin to indent. This is normal, but at this time it is extremely important for the eggs to have adequate ventilation in the incubator; the tiny snakes inside need more oxygen than before.

At the end of incubation—about 60 days—the baby pythons cut a slit in their egg with an egg tooth on the tip of their snout.

The babies will cut a slit, look out, and decide to stay inside the egg, perhaps for as long as a day and a half. Those that leave the egg can be removed to another terrarium and offered water. They should shed within a few weeks, and will eat after shedding.

Don't help: Although this may try your patience, you cannot help the babies out of their eggs. They have to make this step themselves. For unhatched eggs, two days after the rest of the eggs hatch, you can cut a tiny wedge-shaped window into the egg. Lift the wedge gently and peer inside. If a bright-eyed baby snake peers back, replace the egg in the incubator and hope the baby gets the hint. If the baby snake inside is dead, dispose of it. Few clutches have a 100% hatch rate.

HOW-TO: BUILD AN INCUBATOR

Materials needed for one incubator:

• Two wafer thermostat/heaters (obtainable from feed stores; these are commonly used in incubators for chicks)
• One thermometer
• One Styrofoam cooler—one with thick sides (a fish shipping box is ideal)
• One heat tape (reptile-caging heat tape obtainable from pet stores)
• Aluminum tape, to secure the heat tape to the bottom of the Styrofoam

Wide packing tape to use for a hinge between the Styrofoam lid and bottom.

Wire the wafer thermostats in tandem, with about 8" of wire between them, between the heat tape and the wire with the wall plug. Poke two holes, about six or seven inches apart, through the lid of the Styrofoam cooler, and suspend the thermostat/heaters from the inside. Add another hole for a thermometer, so you can check on the inside temperature without opening the top. (If there's no flange on the thermometer to keep it from slipping through the hole in the lid, use a rubber band wound several times around the thermometer to form a flange.) Use wide packing tape to form a hinge along one side of the top, so you can open the incubator and not disturb the wiring between the thermostats and the heat tape.

Arrange the heat tape in a continuous loop over the bottom of the Styrofoam, and tape it into place with aluminum tape.

Close the lid of the cooler, and plug in the thermostat/heaters. Wait half an hour and check the temperature. Adjust the thermostat/heater until the temperature inside the incubator is about 88–90°F (see the species accounts so you'll know what temperature to use). The L-pin "handle" on the top of the thermostat is the rheostat.

Once you have the temperature regulated, put the container of eggs inside the incubator and close the lid.

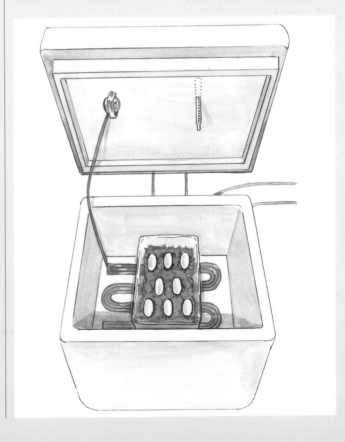

SPECIES ACCOUNTS

The pythons profiled in this chapter were chosen for their tameness, availability, and beauty. Most are small as adults.

Although few hobbyists are prepared to deal with a snake that gets as large as a Burmese python, the "Burm" is included because of its past popularity, calm disposition, and ready availability.

Children's Python Complex
Antaresia spp.

A few hobbyists may remember the Children's Python as *Liasis childreni*, an Australian python with a few subspecies, favored for its exotic origin and small size. Anthony Kluge, a taxonomist from the University of Michigan (Ann Arbor) examined the Children's Python and created a new genus, *Antaresia*, for it. He divided it into four species, separated by geographic distribution and other characteristics. *Antaresia* are all brown pythons, patterned with blotches, and range in size from 18–23"

The Burmese has no natural enemies in the Everglades.

(46–58 cm) for the pygmy python to 69" (175 cm) for the spotted python.

The *Antaresia* have thermosensory pits in their labial scales. Their basic food item is lizards, although some species feed on bats and other warm-blooded prey.

The easiest way to tell the four species apart is by geographic origin, but with the mixes produced by captive breeding programs, coupled with lack of collecting data, determining which species you have (or which species mix) is a challenge.

Blotched Python
Antaresia maculosa

This easy-to-handle small python is the most popular *Antaresia* species in American, Australian, and European collections. It has been bred in captivity for years, which accounts for its availability and popularity.

Appearance: The pale to reddish back of *maculosa* (meaning "spotted") is marked with dark blotches. The dark blotches may join to

form larger blotches or wavy lines along part of the dorsal surface. Unlike other members of *Antaresia*, the blotches remain distinct and sharply defined as the snake matures.

Size: Adults are 43–47" (110–120 cm) and may rarely reach 65" (170 cm).

Range: Eastern and northeastern Australia.

Habitat: Woodland, forest, and semi-arid areas.

Breeding: Females lay large eggs but only 2–12 per clutch. With incubation at 85–90°F (29–33°C), the young emerge in about two months. The hatchlings feed on pinkies.

Care Notes: As with other examples of *Antaresia*, the blotched python lives well in pairs, trios, or as two pairs. The males do not seem to be territorial.

Children's Python
Antaresia childreni

In 1842, John Edward Gray, Keeper of the Zoological Collection at the British Museum, came across a small, nondescript preserved snake from Australia in the collection of the museum. He named the snake *Liasis childreni*, the specific name in honor of his predecessor,

The spotted python is the northeastern representative of Australia's Antaresia *group.*

John G. Children. This is a very small (around three feet), very gentle nocturnal python.

Appearance: Brown splotches dot the red, reddish-brown, or yellow dorsum, but they tend to blend into the background coloration by 3–6 years of age. Along the dorsolateral edge, just above the belly scutes, two lines of dark markings parallel each other to create a paler "stripe" which extends for the first third to half the length of the body. A purple iridescence is evident along the curves of the coils in adults. The underside is paler and unmarked. The tongue is red with gray tips.

Range: North central coastal areas of Australia.

Habitat: Dry woodland, rocky aridlands, and forested areas; coastal plains, grass savannas, along river edges and in large termite mounds. This species is essentially nocturnal, and in the wild it eats bats. It can be found in caves, on a rocky ledge, or hanging by its tail, waiting for its bat prey. It can constrict and eat a bat while hanging from its tailtip. Fortunately, in captivity it accepts prekilled mice.

Size: Adult at just over three feet (1 m); one of the largest recorded was just over 44"(99 cm).

Breeding: Male-female pairs can either be kept together year-round, or maintained separately and placed together in the fall.

A winter cooling period is a natural part of *childreni's* cycle. Withhold food for both the males and female beginning in the late autumn, and reduce the cage temperature to 67–73°F (20–23°C). Daylight hours should be shortened to 8–9 hours. A warm spot (heat tape, heating

Widespread over the Australian continent, large-blotched pythons vary from red through yellow to dark brown.

pad, or spotlight) may or may not be offered (we like to err on the side of caution, and always offer a warm spot) during this 60-to-90-day cooling period.

The gravid females shed 19 days after ovulation, and will lay small numbers (2–12) of rather large eggs 23 days after shedding. The females will use nest boxes filled with damp sphagnum, and will incubate their eggs by coiling around them—be sure the box is large enough to allow this to happen. The usual time for egg deposition is March–May. The eggs will stick to each other but will be less adherent as the hatching date approaches. Incubation generally takes 60 days at 85–90°F (29–33°C).

The young will shed a week or two after hatching and will usually feed on pink mice two to six weeks after shedding. Some hatchlings need to be tempted by scenting the pinky with a lizard.

Stimson's Python
Anteresia stimsoni

Stimson's python, along with the white-lipped python (*Leiopython albertisii*), bears the distinction of having the most teeth—150—of any python species. This small snake with the big dorsal blotches has the widest geographical range in Australia of all the Australian pythons, and its small size has made it popular in captive breeding programs. Like other members of *Antaresia*, Stimson's may seem nippy at first, but settles down with repeated and consistent handling.

Appearance: The base color of the snake is yellow, but the size and close positioning of large maroon blotches make the snake appear dark. Overall there is an enormous range of size, pattern, and color with the Stimson's python; expect some taxonomic splitting of this species in the future. Both sexes bear small thin spurs.

Now four years old, this male anthill python measures only 22 inches.

Both the Stimson's and Children's pythons can be readily distinguished from other small pythons (especially the small-blotched python) by the presence of a distinctive pale lateral line, bordered top and bottom by darker blotches, extending from the neck along the first third to half the length of the body.

Stimson's can be distinguished from the Children's python by its longer snout and larger eyes.

Size: 35–39" (90–100 cm)

Range: This python has a huge range, extending from extreme western throughout central Australia. Its exact distribution over this range has not yet been determined.

Habitat: Stimson's python is found in very arid conditions, on rocky ridges and hillsides, grasslands, and spinifex scrublands. It has been found in termite mounds and caves with resident bat populations, areas that would retain some measure of humidity. The larger eyes may indicate nocturnal activity patterns, a typical behavioral adaptation to desert environments.

Breeding and Care Notes: Stimson's python is relatively new in breeding programs in the United States. Their breeding regimen is much the same as for the other species of *Antaresia*, with reduc-

tion of cage temperature and placing the sexes together in the late fall, copulation from December through March, and egg deposition in April to May. Egg incubation is about 52 days.

Anthill Python
Antaresia perthensis

This small python was formerly known as the pygmy or the Perth python. It lives in termite mounds (called "anthills" in Australia). It feeds primarily on lizards and the rodents found in termite mounds.

Appearance: Yellowish to reddish, with poorly defined blotching. In some examples the blotching may appear as paired markings on each side of the dorsum, but this is not a consistent characteristic. As the snake ages, the blotching becomes less and less distinct. Older animals may appear unicolored. The snout is blunt and rounded.

Range: Pilbara and the adjacent rocky territories in northwest Australia. The specific name, *perthensis*, was chosen because the type specimen was mistakenly identified as being from Perth. In reality, these snakes occur nowhere near Perth.

Habitat: Arid areas in NW Western Australia.

Size: Small, reaching 18–23" (48–56 cm) as an adult. An occasional "sumo" specimen may reach 27".

Breeding: In the wild, this small python not only lives in termitaria but lays its eggs there as well. Captive *perthensis* lay few (2–5) eggs, and the female coils around the clutch. No thermoregulatory shivering has been noted. Incubation at 85–87°F (29–31°C) lasts for 45–60 days before hatchlings emerge. The neonates are small, about 7.5" (190 cm), and evidently feed on small skinks and other lizards.

Care Notes: This small python is extremely hardy and adapts well to captivity. There are records of a 16-year captive life span.

Black-headed Python
Aspidites melanocephalus

The two species in the genus *Aspidites*, the black-headed *A. melanocephalus* and the non-black-headed *A. ramsayi*, are among the most primitive of pythons. Both species are very popular with herpetoculturists, but were until recently practically impossible to acquire. Now, though, both are rather readily available—it merely takes "deep pockets" to become an owner of either species.

Appearance: Black-heads are of variable ground color, but usually are prominently banded snakes. The middorsal area is the darkest, and the straw-yellow and reddish-brown bands are most prominent laterally. The belly is an unrelieved yellow.

Habitat: The black-headed python ranges in suitable areas throughout the northern two-fifths of Australia. It shuns arid lands and deserts, preferring instead the moister coastal forests and woodlands.

Size: Although most are a foot or two or even smaller, black-heads can approach eight feet (244 cm) in total length. They are moderately heavy bodied and are powerful constrictors.

Breeding: Even under captive conditions, this is a late-maturing python. Sexual maturity may not be attained until five years of age or later. For inexplicable reasons, black-headed pythons

Although still very expensive, the interesting black-headed python of north Australia is now readily available to hobbyists.

TIP

Important Fact

One of the most important facts to remember about black-headed pythons is that they are cannibalistic! When you are dealing with a snake that costs in excess of $2,500, this can be critical information.

are still more problematic than the woma. Sustained courtship and breeding activities may still not result in eggs.

Greatest success has been had when winter cooling and photoperiod adjustment have occurred. Combat, at times savage, has been reported between sexually active males. Some breeders feel that such stimulation is important.

In America, where seasons are opposite from those in Australia, black-headed pythons are winter breeders. Eggs are laid through the months of spring and hatching occurs some two to two and a half months following deposition. Small clutches (5–8, rarely a few more)

Unlike this zoo specimen, black-headed pythons are most often encountered in terrestrial situations.

Those that we have had have fed readily on laboratory rodents. In the wild they accept (besides rodents) suitably sized marsupials, ground-nesting birds, lizards, and other snakes, including venomous elapines.

of large eggs are produced. Females often prepare depressions in the substrate for their clutch. Although they may remain with the clutch, they are not known to thermoregulate. Hatchlings are often 20" or more in length.

Black-headed pythons remain among the most expensive of the constricting snakes. Fortunately, they have also proven hardy and undemanding in captivity. They are primarily nocturnal, seeking seclusion during the hours of daylight.

Woma
Aspidites ramsayi

In the 1970s, the Australian woma was virtually unobtainable in the U.S. Today, there are dozens of breeders and the species—although still expensive—is readily available.

Appearance: Variable shades of yellow to tan, with prominent crossbands of darker brown to almost black. These crossbands are narrower than the light bands, and may occasionally have a reddish cast. The ventral surface is paler

A close relative of the black-headed python, the woma is of more southerly distribution and lacks the black head.

Brightly colored as hatchlings (left), adults of the Bismarck ringed python are much duller in color.

than the dorsum. Juveniles can have patches of black on the snout, but the adults do not have black heads. Both sexes bear spurs.

Size: Womas are commonly 5$\frac{1}{2}$ to 6 ft. (168–183 cm), but sometimes grow to eight ft. (244 cm).

Range, Habitat: The woma is firmly associated with semi-arid to desert areas, and with areas that experience a wide range of temperatures. It occurs in a broad east–west band across most of interior Australia, an area of sparse human population.

Breeding: The woma seems easier to breed in captivity than the black-headed python. Nighttime temps should be dropped during the winter cooling period, about 10 degrees lower than the daytime highs. Egg clutch size averages 5–15 eggs. Babies are 16–18" (41–46 cm).

Care Notes: This is a nocturnal snake, and one which prefers to stay on the ground. They may be found during the day in burrows of small mammals (one of their favored prey items), or in hollowed logs or inside hollowed trees. In nature they dine on mammals, birds, lizards, and other snakes.

Womas are, by and large, calm and docile snakes. Once stimulated by fear or the scent of food, they have the habit of biting and being slow to let go. If you are bitten, give the snake time to make up its mind to turn loose.

Ringed Python
Bothrochilus boa

The Bismarck ringed python is a fairly small, mild-mannered, agreeable python. It needs fairly high humidity in the adult's enclosure, in the incubator, and in the hatchling's shoeboxes or other housing.

Appearance: If young ringed pythons retained their clownlike colors and patterns into adulthood, this would be the world's favorite python, hands-down. The hatchlings are bright orange, dotted intermittently with large black spots. The spots in many places are big enough to form bands which circle the entire body, and a green iridescent "glaze" can be seen in the bends of the coils.

But after about six months, those from the western part of the range dull from orange to olive green, and the black dots become less obvious. The venter is light yellow. Snakes from the eastern part of the range tend to retain the ringed or banded appearance, but it dulls.

Range: Bismarck Islands, off the coast of Papua New Guinea.

Habitat: Forests, open land, cultivated areas. May be nocturnal.

Size: This medium-sized python may be from 3–6 ft. (0.95–1.73 m).

Breeding: These snakes are best sexed by probing, since there are no distinct external characteristics. Males probe from three to four times deeper than the females' probe depth of 2–3 scales.

The Houston Zoo has used both photoperiod and temperature manipulation to induce breeding. Summertime day length is increased up to 14 hours, with daytime temps in the mid-80s F (26–30°C) and mid-to-upper 70s F (24–26°C) at night. As daylight hours are reduced, incrementally reduce daytime and nightime temperatures by 10° and 15°F, respectively. After two months at the lowest level of light and heat, begin to increase both the temperature and daylength incrementally to summertime levels.

The females generally breed from December to March, and will lay their clutches after about 60 days of gestation, in March through July. Artificial incubation at 90°F (33°C) will take about 60 days, with the young emerging in April through September.

Care Notes: Most ringed pythons will have difficulty in shedding if not permitted to soak and/or if their cage is too dry. The cage should have a hot spot.

These snakes like to have a hiding box, and will use it especially if they are startled by something outside their cage or if they feel nervous. If startled when constricting or feeding, they will leave the food item and not return to it. These snakes have proportionately small heads for their size, and prefer smaller rats or mice. Young or hatchlings may eat lizards and small frogs; those reluctant to take a pinkie may do so if the item is scented with a lizard or frog. Two neonates at the Houston Zoo preferentially ate freshwater fish, including goldfish. You need to be aware that many herpetoculturists do not advocate the sustained feeding of goldfish to any reptile.

White-lipped Python
Leiopython albertisii

There are three different color phases of the bad-tempered white-lipped (formerly known as the D'Albert's) python. These are such attractive snakes that dedicated hobbyists or professional herpetoculturists cannot resist working with them. As a result, there are now some good techniques available for handling the adults and the young.

As with many other species of pythons, the captive-born young seem to adjust more easily than the adults to handling, but that may be because more keepers are willing to be bitten by a two-foot snake than an eight-foot snake, and so handle the smaller snakes more. Whenever the size of the snake does not preclude it, use a snake hook to lift the python, then transfer it to your hand. This tends to avoid the bite-first-and-then-look response to an encroaching human hand.

No matter its body color, the white-lipped python is aptly named.

The neonates are nervous, jumpy snakes that need easily accessed hiding areas (they will burrow into a substrate of wood shavings, which helps provide the impression of seclusion).

Appearance: The white-lipped may be solid black with white lips; gray, usually with a darker head and dark-peppered cream-colored labials; and the typical form, with a dark back, golden flanks, black head, and dark-spotted white lips. This last form almost seems to glow when seen in the woods or in its cage.

The variety in coloration indicates that we are looking at a species complex, rather than a single species. All three forms have soft, smooth skin, and gray to gray-brown eyes. They have large heads with expanded temporal regions. The tongue is blue-gray with reddish sides and tip.

Size: 7–8 ft. (213–243 cm); the black morphs reach 9 ft. (274 cm). Hatchlings are 15″ (38 cm).

Origin: Northern islands of Torres Strait, off the northern coast of Australia; New Guinea, in elevations of less than 6,250 ft. (1,250 m). An isolated population is found on the island of Mussau, an island on the tip of the Bismarck Archipelago.

Range/Habitat: The white-lipped python is found in rainforests, swamps, and grasslands, near water. Nocturnal, it may be seen on roadsides, especially after a rain.

Breeding: Some breeders have found the white-lipped python needs large diurnal temperature variations to breed, with daytime highs of 92°F (33°C) and nighttime lows of 70°F (21°C).

The sexes are placed together in January. No temperature fluctuations other than the 92/70 regimen are employed, and the 12/12 day/night schedule is unchanged. Females begin to show signs of being gravid in March or April, and the males are removed from the cages at that time. Eight to 15 eggs are laid from March–June.

The often feisty white-lipped python occurs in a black or, as shown here, a bronze phase.

After about 60 days of incubation, the hatchlings emerge. It is best to house each one separately. Some time (6–8 weeks) needs to elapse before the young are hungry; a few may wait 3–4 months before feeding on their own. Try a fuzzy mouse; reluctant feeders may be further tempted with a skink or gecko.

Care Notes: Be sure you keep the hatchlings warm enough; they need to be kept above 80°F for at least their first six months.

Care Notes: The humidity-adapted white-lipped may have trouble shedding its entire skin. If patches of the old skin adhere, a 2–3 hour soak in warm to tepid water will loosen those portions so that they can be removed. Captives offered a hide box filled with damp sphagnum will spend a great deal of time in the box; the Barkers of Vida Preciosa, Inc. have noted the improved skin conditions of the white lips offered this option.

Water Pythons
Liasis sp.
All 3 *Liasis* species discussed here are fairly small pythons with an affinity for water. (One member of this genus, the olive python, is not included in this book. Its adult size of 15 feet and perfectly foul disposition qualifies it as a snake we don't recommend).

The *Liasis* are nervous pythons, needing a hide box or hiding area on a consistent basis. Both the brown water python and the Macklot's python tend to be nippy, although most herpetoculturists point out that gentle, frequent handling helps calm these snakes. The Savu python is more easygoing.

The water pythons feed on mice and other rodents.

Brown Water Python
Liasis fuscus
Not everyone loves the brown water python, mostly due to its edgy disposition, but it is frequently found on dealers' lists. Both young and adults will calm with handling, and for this snake, calming makes sense—it tends to defecate as it thrashes around, liberally coating everything within range.

Appearance: Brown to brownish black, paling to yellow cream on the venter. The chin is white. The dorsum has an opalescent sheen.

Size: Females average just under five feet, and the males average out at 51". A big example will reach eight feet. Hatchlings are 16" (42 cm).

Range: The northern edge of Australia, eastern Irian Jaya, and western Papua.

Habitat: Near water, eating whatever warm-blooded prey (waterfowl, rats) it encounters. Females also seek out and eat the eggs of water geese.

Breeding: These snakes breed from November through January, when day temps are 97–89°F (30–33°C) and 60–64°F (16–18°C) at night. Eight to 12 eggs are deposited from January–March, and young emerge from March to June. The female may or may not heat the eggs by shivering. Under artificial incubation, eggs hatch in 59–63 days at 88–90°F (31–33°C). The Barkers have found their young "browns" will feed voluntarily when four months old.

Macklot's Python
Liasis mackloti

Although some herpetoculturists feel that Macklot's and the brown water python are the same species, we feel they are distinct species, based on geographical distribution and physical characteristics.

Appearance: Macklot's python is dark brown green above, paling to ocher laterally and white ventrally. The white coloration extends up onto the upper and lower labials. The eyes are gray.

Size: Up to 6 feet (1.8 m).

Range: Southeast Indonesia.

Breeding: Male Macklot's engage in male-to-male sparring during the fall to winter breeding season, even if no female is around, so keep the males in their own cages when they are not with the female. Breeding usually takes place during the night. Gravid females fast until after egg deposition.

The brown water python of Australia and New Guinea is of moderate size and lacks any brilliant colors.

Eight to 14 eggs are laid from April until early June. Females will incubate the eggs and will maintain a 85–88°F (29–30°C) by shivering. If the cage temperature is 88° or higher, the female will loosen her coils and not shiver. Incubation is 56–60 days.

Macklot's python, a semi-aquatic Indonesian species, has a variable disposition.

Care notes: These snakes do well in captivity but seem susceptible to eye and respiratory infections. These are high-humidity snakes, and careful attention needs to be paid to humidity and to cage cleanliness.

Savu Python
Liasis mackloti savuensis
Size: To perhaps five feet (152 cm) in length. This python is sexually mature at about three feet.
Range: Known only from the island of Savu (100 miles west of Timor).
Habitat: Woodlands.
Appearance: The hatchlings are a brilliant terra cotta dorsally and white ventrally. The dorsum darkens with growth and age, creating an olive gray adult. The eyes are stark white.

The Savu python is a small species that is dull when adult.

The spectacular, rare, and expensive Boelen's python has proven very difficult to breed in captivity.

Breeding: Three to five large eggs. The usual regimen of separating the sexes, cooling, reuniting the sexes and misting/warming seems to work. Incubation is for about 60 days at 88°F (30°C).

Captive hardiness: The Savu python has proven a hardy, ideally sized, good-tempered captive, feeding readily on mice.

Boelen's Python
Morelia boeleni

This snake is one of the most protected animals in Papua New Guinea. Only recently has it become available, and the few Boelen's that do appear on lists command prices in the several-thousand-dollar range. Although several zoos and private breeding institutions are working with this snake, reproductive strategies are still being determined.

Appearance: This is a stocky python with a big, wide head which is distinct from the narrow neck. The snake is a shimmering blue-black on the dorsum, and pale lemon yellow ventrally. The labials are vertically barred with black and yellow, giving a toothy-smile look to the snake at first glance. To add to the contrast, a series of narrow yellow bars jut upwards on each side from the belly, but do not connect over the back. The underbelly darkens posteriorly to black.

Origin: New Guinea

Habitat: Rainforest above 3,280 ft. (1,000 m), in humid, low-light conditions. At these elevations Boelen's are a cool temperature python.

Size: A heavy-bodied 6–9 ft. (1.83–2.4 m). A maximum size has not been reported, but is probably 10 feet.

Breeding: Some of the first Boelen's pythons in the U.S. were maintained at the Dallas Zoo, but without breeding success. Now at least eight U.S. zoos have active breeding programs for these snakes.

Small numbers of Boelen's pythons are in private breeding collections such as VPI and Stone Mountain. A few breeding successes have been

Hatchling diamond pythons do not bear the intricate patterns of the adults.

reported. The young are quite different in appearance from the adults, being reddish with white markings. Clutch size runs from 9–16 eggs.

Care Notes: Captive Boelen's feed on laboratory rodents and small rabbits. Examples from the wild are thought to include ground-nesting birds in their diet.

These high-humidity snakes may have trouble shedding in lower humidity conditions, and misting the snake or increasing the humidity of the cage just before shedding may aid in the process. Although usually encountered in terrestrial conditions, Boelen's spotted in the wild have shown an amazing ability to climb.

Carpet Pythons
Morelia spilota ssp.

The carpet pythons are Australian and New Guinean pythons which are divided into six

subspecies, only three of which will be described here. Only two of these, the coastal and jungle carpets, are seen with any frequency in the United States. A third subspecies, the diamond python, is one of the most coveted of all snakes in American herpetoculture. Breeding techniques and behavior patterns of all the subspecies are essentially the same.

Diamond Python
M. s. spilota

The diamond python is a small (about 6 ft./ 188 cm) slender species from eastern New South Wales.

Appearance: "Diamonds" are black snakes with yellow tipping on dorsal and lateral scales. Yellow diamonds are enclosed in patches of jet black on the sides. The subspecies is cream to yellow ventrally. Hatchlings of any carpet python subspecies look very much alike.

Size: Adults range from 6–7½ ft. (188–229 cm).

Range: Australia, from the eastern part of New South Wales.

Habitat: Forest edges, forest clearings, river edges, and rocky ledges, where they feed on small rodents and marsupials. During the winter, diamond pythons are commonly found near or in human dwellings in New South Wales. They may be underneath or in the rafters of poultry sheds, or in the attics or crawl spaces of homes.

Breeding: Within their range, there is a notable variation in seasonal temperature. Some summer days reach into the 90s F (33–35°C), and winter temps can drop to freezing (0°C). Both sexes are inactive during cold weather, seeking shelter on the coldest days and on most nights. The winter shelter can be in human dwellings, but more frequently is on sunny, north-oriented escarpments.

In the spring, the males begin prowling, looking for sexually receptive females. The males may wander considerable distances in this process. Once they encounter a female, mating occurs and the males begin wandering again.

The gravid females use their neck, curved in a J-shape, to scrape together a nest of leaves. They deposit their eggs in the debris. Females coil around their eggs in the leaves, only leaving to warm up in a patch of sun before returning and re-coiling around the eggs.

Diamonds lay clutches of up to 50 eggs, although 16–25 is more normal. Incubation of 88–92°F (31–34°C) seems to be the norm, with eggs hatching in about 60 days.

Termed a jungle carpet python, the carpet pythons of northeastern Australia are quite brightly colored.

Care Notes: Diamond pythons like seclusion, both on the floor of the cage and in an elevated hide box. They will eat a variety of small rodents. Adults are fairly docile; the young are nippy until they settle down to a routine and become more adept at identifying food and enemies. The young may not recognize pinkies as food; try jumpers (furred young mice with the eyes barely open) instead.

Jungle Carpet Python
Morelia s. cheynei

The jungle carpet python has the smallest range of the species. They are fairly small, slender-bodied, with large heads. Their background coloration is pale, with black-edged dark blotches alternating with the paler yellow-to-cream base color. The overall effect is a banded pattern. The eyes are dark and the tongue is blue.

The jungle carpets don't seem to get more than 5½ feet (140 cm) long, although some examples from the Atherton rainforest may reach more than 8 ft. (250 cm). Captive-maintained specimens may reach a greater size than wild examples, but the lineage of most captive carpet pythons is too muddled to identify the exact subspecies.

The rivers and waterways that drain Australia's Atherton Tableland form the heart of the range of the jungle carpet python. They like dense subtropical rainforest, but much of the rainforest in the tableland area has been reduced to disjunct corridors. Within their preferred habitat, the jungle pythons are arboreal. In captivity, they mate and feed from elevated perches.

The breeding regime is much like that for other carpets, including wintertime cooling and reduction of the photoperiod. Re-introduction of the sexes is followed by copulation, basking, and ovulation. Egg deposition is about 40 days after ovulation, and hatching occurs about 54 days after deposition. The young are 16" (42 cm) at hatching. Some breeders separate the sexes, but we have not found it necessary in Florida.

Coastal Carpet Python
Morelia s. mcdowelli

This is the largest and most varied of the carpet pythons, and is one of the most commonly available in the United States.

The coastal carpet is dark dorsally, paler ventrally, with 60–80 dark-edged pale blotches arranged evenly from head to tail. The labials are pale to white, but the head pattern is indistinct.

The coastal carpet ranges from 6–8 ft. (182–244 cm). On rare occasions, some may reach 14 ft. (427 cm), but there's a strong

The striped phase of the coastal carpet python is just one of many color phases now available.

selection against snakes living long enough to grow that large.

The snake is found along coastal New South Wales, from the Cape York Peninsula to Coffs Harbor at the southern boundary of that state. It is most commonly encountered in heavily timbered areas, indicating its arboreal tendencies, or in the upper rafters of buildings, especially those with chickens within, indicating a preferred dietary item.

Breeding techniques include wintertime cooling and photoperiod reduction. When the female is observed to ovulate, or begin to bask with the lower half of her body turned upwards, the male is removed. Egg deposition of about 27 eggs occurs 44 days after ovulation or 25 days after the final shed. Incubation takes about 54 days, and can be as warm as 87–89°F (31–32°C).

A portrait of a Wamena locale green tree python.

Chondro Python
Morelia viridis

Known for years as *Chondropython viridis*, the scientific name of the chondro was changed in 1994 to *Morelia viridis* to reflect its close relationship with that species. But the common name of "chondro" persists, and hobbyists and professionals alike have continued to use it.

Some hobbyists might consider this snake a choice python due to its attractive appearance and manageable adult size, but its cost, snappy temperament, and specialized regimen of care make it a snake for the experienced keeper who doesn't mind being bitten on a consistent basis.

Appearance: The most typical adult phase of the chondro is a bright green with a series of white or blue dorsal and lateral spots. Blue or yellow examples are highly prized; chondros from Aru island are a deeper green coloration with powder-blue lips and venter.

Hatchlings may be brick-red, lemon yellow, or brown (even within the same clutch), with the characteristic intermittent white markings along the back. Most change to the bright green of the adult by the time they are two years old. A few chondros remain solid lemon yellow or blue their entire lives (see "A Chondro by Any Other Name" on page 50). All have thermosensory pits along the upper and lower labials.

TIP

Chondros' Needs
This is an arboreal snake that needs branches, not pieces of PVC piping, to hang from. It needs warm temperatures and high humidity to feed.

This is a hatchling green tree python from the Wamena locale.

Size: Usually maxes out at six feet (180 cm), and rarely gets to seven feet (210 cm). This is a fairly slender snake, so a specimen coiled cinnamon-bun style across a branch may appear smaller than it actually is.

Range: Chondro pythons are found in Papua New Guinea and in the Cape York Peninsula of Australia.

Habitat: These arboreal snakes are found in elevations from sea level to 6,000 ft. (1,850 m), which encompasses a wide range of habitat niches. Although these agile snakes are certainly arboreal, there's an increasing body of evidence that they ground-forage at night. During the day, sleeping chondros can be found in sheltered tree-hollows, secreted inside bromeliads, or on low branches 20" (0.5 m)

above the ground. Unfortunately, wild-caught chondros arrive at the dealers without specific collection data, so replication of the original habit is at best guesswork.

Breeding: A great many of the chondros on the market today are the result of captive breeding. Generally, chondros breed from late August to late December. Do not place two males together with the female; they will engage in male—male combat with serious damage to each other and anything else in the way at the time. A chondro bite is painful and impressive—not only from the discomfort involved in gently peeling back the snake's jaws so that you won't pull out any of its teeth, but also in the quantity of blood shed.

Eight to 12 eggs are laid from late November through February, sometimes in late April. Females need an elevated egg deposition box. Those not given elevated boxes will sometimes drop their eggs while draped across a treelimb.

Incubation, either maternal or artificial, is variable, from 39 to 65 days. If the female is permitted maternal incubation, she will coil around the eggs. In northern areas, she will begin thermoregulatory contractions if the cage temperature falls below 84°F (28°C).

Monitor the actions of the female to ensure the eggs don't dry out. If you prefer to place the eggs in an incubator, be certain that ventilation is adequate, particularly during the last few weeks of incubation. Some breeders now feel that a slight drop in incubation temperature during the last week of incubation provides the "time to come out" stimulus, the lack of which otherwise results in full-term eggs that inexplicably fail to hatch.

Young chondros seem very susceptible to irreversible tail kinking. The problem is evidently due to delicate vertebrae in the tail, which can be dislocated by simple actions such as immobilizing the tailtip when using a probe to determine the snake's sex or during manual eversion of the hemipenes on a hatchling.

Newborn chondros can be difficult feeders, but generally can be started on pinkie mice. If they resist the pinkies, try starting them on lizards or frogs. Attaching a few chicken feathers to the pink mouse might be helpful. Adults will feed on birds (chicks) or on rodents.

Hatchling green tree pythons from a single clutch may be yellow, red, maroon, or chocolate.

Blood Pythons
Python curtus ssp.

There are three species in the blood python group, also known as short-tailed pythons. The best known is the black blood python, *Python curtus*; less known but equally interesting are the red blood python, *P. brongersmai*, and the Borneo short-tailed python, *P. bretsteini*.

These snakes are geographically isolated from each other but are still closely related (some experts view *bongersmai* and *curtus* as subspecies of *Python curtus*, and *P. breitsteini* as a distinct species). Their care regimen is much alike. We'll use the red blood python as our primary example.

Red Blood Python
Python brongersmai

Most of the beautifully patterned and colored blood pythons exported from Sumatra leave that country as skins, not as pets. Each year, some 60,000 of the darker morphs are turned into shoes, boots, belts, purses, and

clothing. Several hundred of the brighter red morphs, the ones for whom the common name "blood" was coined, are exported annually for the pet trade.

Appearance: At first glance, the red blood python looks like an outrageously obese snake. At second glance you notice the beautifully mottled blotches of red, orange, yellow, and tan, and the paler blotches on the sides. The lighter blotches on the sides are peppered with minute black dots. The head is flat and large. The tongue is usually black. The eyes are small, and in the red blood python, no small rows of scales (called "suboculars") separate the eye from the upper labials. In both the other species, the lower edge of the eye is separated from the upper labials by a ring of smaller scales, the suboculars. Only the red blood python has the characteristic red coloration; both the other subspecies are mottled in shades of brown, tan, and gray.

Size: Red blood pythons are sexually mature at 3½–4 ft. (108–122 cm). Larger snakes may reach 10 ft. (304 cm). Hatchlings are 12 to 16 in. (30–41 cm).

The Borneo short-tailed python and the Sumatran short-tailed python are smaller, never exceeding five feet (152 cm). Their hatchlings are just slightly smaller than the blood python, at 10 to 13" (25–32 cm).

Range: The red blood python is found over much of SE Asia in Bangkok, Banga Island, the islands of Singapore, Pinang, and north and central Sumatra.

The Borneo short-tailed python is found on the island of Borneo, and the black blood python is found in southern and western Sumatra.

Habitat: These snakes spend at least part of their time in marshy areas with high humidity, and of all the pythons, seem to need these conditions duplicated for successful husbandry. Blood pythons are extremely susceptible to repeated respiratory infections if their caging is too small or not humid enough.

Breeding: Although young and hatchling Borneo and Sumatran short-tailed pythons are available, not much work has been done specifically on their captive propagation. Until it is, it seems likely that the guidelines used in breeding the red blood python could be successfully extrapolated.

In North America, red blood pythons mate from January to April. Although temperature fluctuations play a role in triggering this behavior, this snake seems to require less of a fluctuation than some other python species. Instead, the key is day length.

Python curtus *is now known as the black blood python.*

Once considered a subspecies of the blood python, Python curtus, P. brongersmai *is now a full species and is referred to as the red blood python.*

During the summer, day lengths need to be about 15 hours. Begin decreasing to nine hours of daylight (see page 31 for this technique).

As the days are decreased, begin cooling. Most breeders use a "cool" daytime temperature of 83-85°F (28-29°C), and a nighttime temperature in the high 70s F (24-25°C). A hot spot may or may not be utilized, but it seems prudent to offer the pythons a choice in thermoregulation.

Some breeders either drastically reduce the number and size of feedings from early December until March, or stop feeding the animals altogether during this time. Snakes should be placed together in late December or January. They can be left with each other, or simply removed and reintroduced periodically.

With the cooling period's end in February, the snakes' cage can be warmed to 86-88°F (29-32°C) in the day and 78-82°F (26-28°C) during the night.

Copulation may occur numerous times; keep track of the dates, so you'll know when to expect eggs. Successful copulation is indicated by ovulation, which occurs in March to April. The mid-body bulge is apparent for 24 hours.

Eggs are laid about 60 days after mating. Although the female Borneo short-tailed python (*P. breitensteini*) will incubate her eggs with thermoregulatory shivering, this has not yet been observed with the red blood python or the black blood python. The eggs hatch in 58–65 days.

Neonates shed much later than most python young, at 8–12 weeks. Although the young may feed before that first ecdysis, some breeders feel it unnecessary to offer food until the young are 4 weeks old and show an active interest in eating.

Care Notes: The important thing to remember when providing caging for a blood python—or indeed any short-tailed python—is to be guided more by the animal's weight, not its comparatively small size. Make sure that the cage is at least twice as long as the snake, and broad enough so it can turn around. Being able to move around as desired seems to help avoid the respiratory infections that are chronic problems with blood pythons.

Another respiratory preventative seems to be humidity. Red blood pythons do best in high-humidity cages, but good ventilation is a must. Reluctant feeders (usually adults from the wild) can sometimes be cajoled into feeding by duplicating the marshy environment where they

Rather than being referred to as a blood python, **Python breitensteini** *is now called the Borneo short-tailed python.*

ambush-feed in the wild. This can be done by providing a damp humus substrate (enough to burrow in), a large soaking bowl, and a hide-box.

These are primarily nocturnal snakes, quiescent during the day and active (and feeding) during the night. Captives feed on rodents, small mammals, and birds.

Burmese Pythons
Python molurus ssp.

The Burmese python group is actually three big snakes—the Burmese (known affectionately as the "Burm"), the Indian, and the Ceylon pythons. All are subspecies of *Python molurus*, but each has its own common name and its own coterie of hobbyists. Of the three, the Burmese is the best-known and most popular.

The gentle and docile nature of the Burmese—in addition to its beauty—is the main reason for its popularity as a pet or breeder snake. The downside is that the snake gets BIG, and a big snake is more than the average hobbyist can handle. A well-fed hatchling Burm will be seven feet at the end of the first year, and easily 10 feet at the end of year two. Lawmakers everywhere in the U.S. are very nervous about big snakes, and a young Burm just two years old may not be legal where you live. A snake that is 10 feet long or longer is too large (read "too heavy and too dangerous") to be handled by one person.

Think before you Burm: There's no secondary market for a snake 10 ft. or longer. Zoos and nature centers already have their big snakes—and they won't take another even if it's free. If you give it away, you have no assurance that your former pet will be well treated. You may still be legally liable, should something happen. Turning it loose is not an option, period. The only option may be euthanization, hardly a course of action a snake hobbyist would want.

Appearance: The normal coloration of the Burmese python is tan with dark-edged olive-brown dorsal and lateral blotches. A dark spear-head is present on the top of the head. This used to be the standard (and only) color pattern of the Burmese, but that has changed radically. Captive breeding programs have created many aberrant patterns and colors.

Size: Adult at 7–10 feet (213–335 cm), commonly attains 14 ft. (426 cm), and has been recorded at over 25 ft. (762 cm) long. Hatchlings are about 16" (41 cm). This is a heavy-bodied snake, and the females tend to grow to a much larger size than the males.

Range: Burma, Malaysia, and Indonesia.

Habitat: The Burmese python is found in open fields, cultivated areas, and wooded areas. It is an adept swimmer.

Breeding: Before you breed your Burm, be certain you have a market for all 50+ of the young (or plan to destroy the excess eggs). Male Burms are sexually mature at a seven-foot length; the females at 10 ft.

Successful breeding of the Burmese pythons may be as easy as placing the males and females together after cycling them. If no response is shown, gently mist the snakes in the evening.

The female, when gravid, will put on considerable girth. Increase her feedings, both in size and frequency. Make sure that an egg deposition box, big enough for the female, the substrate, and the eggs, is inside the enclosure. The Burmese, in keeping with its size, lays large

The huge Burmese python is now established in Florida's Everglades and surrounding regions.

clutches of large eggs. Up to 60 eggs are laid each time.

Females will readily incubate their eggs, if allowed, and will coil around the eggs and raise the clutch's temperature by shivering. Artificial incubation is, for most breeders, less worrisome than watching over and trying to second-guess the female. Use the standardized temperatures and incubation length suggested on page 57.

Care Notes: This docile snake feeds well on mice, rats, rabbits, and chickens or other birds.

Indian Python
Python m. molurus

The Indian python (also called the Indian rock python) is the nominate form of *Python molurus*, meaning it was the first described. Because it is a protected form (Appendix I, CITES) it is not a common pet trade python. Indian pythons cannot be taken over state lines for commercial purposes without special permits, but they can be sold commercially within that state with no restrictions. Most dealers avoid large pythons, especially those needing federal paperwork.

Appearance: Lighter in overall coloration than the Burmese, the Indian python also lacks the Burmese-definitive arrowhead on top of the head.

Size: Adult at smaller sizes than the Burmese, the Indian is sexually mature at 8–12 ft. (282–366 cm). Some examples may reach 15 ft. (457 cm) or more. This is still a large snake.

Range: India, West Pakistan to Nepal; Sri Lanka.

Habitat: Like the Burmese, the Indian python frequents open fields and forested areas. It stays near permanent bodies of water, and is adept at swimming and climbing.

Breeding: Mating occurs from November through March. Clutch size is usually smaller than the Burmese, but more than 40 eggs have been reported. Egg deposition occurs from February to early June, with hatching from April to early August. Incubation follows the standard procedure on page 56.

Care Notes: Because this is a federally designated endangered species, interstate or international sale or exchange requires permits. However, if the Indian python has been intergraded with the Burmese or the Ceylon race at some time in the past, no permits are required. You may be asked to prove this intergradation.

The disposition of the Indian python varies by individual and circumstances. Most quiet with repeated gentle handling.

Ceylon Python
Python m. pimbura

The validity of the Ceylon python is a moot point, according to many taxonomists. This is a smallish large python, reaching a length of 10–11 ft. (305–335 cm). It is found only on the island of Ceylon (Sri Lanka). In appearance it resembles the Indian python most closely, but is perhaps a little more intensely colored. It does not come under the regulations which encumber its cogeneric the Indian python (*P. m. molurus*), which makes it very attractive to hobbyists and dealers, for obvious reasons. The Burmese described on dealers' lists as "dwarf Burmese" resemble (superficially at least) this python.

Ball Python
Python regius

The ball python is arguably the most popular and easily kept of the pythons. Add to that the snake's small adult size (less than six feet when full grown), its adaptability to captive life and gentle handling, and a new set of captive-bred

The endangered Indian rock python cannot be sold across state lines without a federal permit.

The Ceylon (Sri Lankan) rock python is intermediate in color between the Indian rock python and the Burmese python.

color morphs, and you can understand why for many people the only python is the ball python, *Python regius.*

The ball python was named for its habit of coiling in a tight ball when frightened, with its head in the center and protected by the body coils. As the snake becomes more accustomed to captivity, this behavior lessens and finally disappears. Some captive-born examples may not exhibit the coiling behavior, because these snakes haven been handled since birth. The ball python's shyness/good disposition and ready availability in the wild have made it a very popular pet store snake, with tens of thousands being imported from Africa each year. But not all of these snakes are imported as adults; in fact, these are mostly imported as hatchlings.

In Africa, snake hunters seek out the gravid female ball pythons. These are sold to the animal dealer, who holds the females until they deposit their eggs. Then females are then shipped out to the pet market, and the eggs held until the babies hatch. Those babies are then shipped out, to appear a few weeks later on the lists of wholesalers in the U.S.

Appearance: The normal coloration of the ball python is a pretty combination of warm tan blotches over a black ground color. The snake's head is distinct from its neck, even though this is a heavy-bodied snake. Labial pits are present, and are most evident towards the tip of the nose.

The enormous popularity of the ball python has meant a number of serious captive breeding programs. In addition to the normal phase, there are ivory, piebald, leucistic, albino, axanthic, bumblebee, spider, spinner blast, and pewter phases being bred.

Range: Western Africa.

Habitat: This basically terrestrial snake is found in western tropical Africa. It lives in scrub and semi-aridland areas. It is a hunter, following rodent and other small animal prey far back into their burrows. Although not a tree-dwelling snake, it can climb quite well.

Size: Hatchlings are about 9" (21 cm) long; adults range from about three and a half feet to six feet (90–182 cm).

Breeding: Ball pythons can be sexed by comparing the size of the spurs. Males generally have longer spurs. Probing is a more effective way to determine sex; males will probe to six subcaudal scales, the females to three.

Once you have a pair, a trio, or even two pair, separate the sexes and use the standard cycling approach described on page 46 to ready them for breeding. During the cooling period, reduce the humidity in the cage by replacing the water bowl with a smaller one. Maintain a daytime

TIP

A Python of Any Other Name

Don't buy a ball python color morph without research. Those who breed these snakes tend to make up their own names for their color morphs.

Known as the royal python to hobbyists in other parts of the world, in the United States the name ball python was coined and found favor because of its habit of balling tightly when startled.

temperature of 76–80°F (25–27°C) and a night-time low of 68–70°F (19–21°C).

At the end of the cooling period, begin to elevate the temperatures to their normal summer levels and place the sexes together. If you have a second male, he can be added temporarily to stimulate breeding activity. After the territorial defense behavior, remove the second male. Copulation should take place. If you have two pairs, the first male can be used to initiate breeding activity with the second pair.

If the snakes do not breed, separate them and try again in a week. Sometimes several introductions are necessary before breeding takes place.

Ovulation occurs from mid-March through April. Gravid females darken in color, a process thought to increase the body temperature when thermoregulating by basking. Gravid females may also bask with the posterior portion of the body turned upside down, under the cage's hotspot.

In the wild, ball pythons may deposit their eggs in the moist, humid burrows of small mammals. Temperatures in these burrows can be in the low 90s F (32–34°C) with an 85 percent humidity. In captivity, they will enter an egg deposition box and deposit small clutches of large eggs.

Incubation takes about two months at a temperature of 87–90°F (31–32°C), and humidity needs to be about 85–95 percent.

If you choose maternal incubation, maintain cage temperatures at 85–89°F (29–32°C). Watch the female. If she uncoils from her eggs and

Everglades Pythons

The Everglades National Park is one of the busiest National Parks in the nation. Located at the southern tip of Florida, this subtropical park is comprised of more than a million and a quarter acres of swampland, sloughs, hammocks, and marl prairies. Cars filled with birders, canoers, campers, fishing enthusiasts, butterfly watchers, and sightseers sweep southward from Homestead to Flamingo, stopping periodically to read the informative roadside signs, train binoculars on a short-tailed hawk or white crowned pigeon, or view an alligator. Most of these visitors never realize they have visited the known habitat of a very large and very unwanted Asian interloper—the Burmese python.

Tales of pythons in Florida have been told at least since the 1970s. But then, the evidence was based on one or two pythons being found each year, and they were thought to be recently escaped pets. At that time no one seemed to even consider that a python would actually become established. But as the years passed the findings became more frequent, and some of the snakes being found were larger. The largest yet reported and authenticated was a 20-foot, 200-lb., reticulated python captured alive by biologists in Ft. Lauderdale.

By the late '90s, adult and hatchling Burms had been documented. By 2003 breeding by this snake in the Everglades had been documented. One female managed to successfully incubate a large clutch of eggs beneath an overturned wheelbarrow next to a park maintenance building.

Today (2009) it is actually difficult to miss seeing one or more Burmese pythons crossing the park roadways on warm, humid nights during spring, summer, and early autumn. It is not unusual to find this big predator crossing both paved and marl roads from the southern border of Lake Okeechobee to the tip of the Florida peninsula.

With the large number of pythons now present in the wilds of South Florida, it is entirely possible for an enthusiastic hobbyist to see (or even to collect) a python of his or her own. Because all wildlife is protected in the park itself, no harassment or collection is allowed within the confines of the park. Pythons outside the park boundaries are fair game—but remember that a feral 10-foot long biting, constricting, Burmese python can be a formidable adversary. Do not attempt to collect one if you are alone.

leaves them, transfer them to your own incubator and take over the incubation process.

Care Notes: This python has been sold as the ultimate pet snake. Its gentle disposition, attractive appearance, and modest adult size are all contributory reasons for this viewpoint.

The downside of ball python ownership is the reluctance of some examples to feed, and this may be partially explained by the Barkers' work with this snake. In Africa, they found, young ball pythons climb trees to feed on bird hatchlings, and the adults feed on what are commonly called gerbils—but these are a different species than what is found in our pet stores. If your ball python is reluctant to feed on lab mice, offer gerbils, adult rats, rat pups, guinea

Ball pythons of normal coloration remain the most inexpensive and readily available to hobbyists.

pigs, hamsters, or white-footed mice (we live-trapped a half-dozen and began raising them ourselves). Try the prey items in different colors and both dead and alive. Sometimes exposing the brain of the prey item and leaving it in the doorway of the hide box will tempt your ball python to feed.

The Institute for Herpetological Research has found that a hide box made from an inverted clay flowerpot will sometimes provide a secure enough hiding spot to induce a ball python to feed. They enlarged the drain hole (using pliers to nip out the edges of the drain hole until it was large enough) and placed the flowerpot upside down in the cage. The ball python would rest inside the flowerpot and peer out the enlarged drain hole to watch its potential prey item. IHR found the combination of this secure hiding area and offering live mice as food was one way to break the ball python's self-imposed

fast. If you do try this technique, do not leave the mouse in the cage overnight; it is not uncommon for live food items such as rodents to eat portions of their supposed predator at night.

Timor Python
Python timorensis

Timor pythons are only rarely available in the pet market. They remain one of the most difficult pythons to breed in captivity.

Appearance: Although the overall color may vary somewhat, the pattern of the Timor python is rather standard. These pythons are most heavily patterned anteriorly and may be unicolored posteriorly. The ground color can vary from straw or olive, to a rather bright yellow and may be more brilliant by day than at night. The color of the pattern is a dark brown.

═══ TIP ═══

Difficult?

Timors are not difficult snakes to keep, but they have proven difficult to cycle reproductively. It is fortunate that they are small, for they usually have rather feisty personalities and do not hesitate to strike far and accurately if bothered. Most secrete urates and feces if handled.

Anteriorly, the snake may appeared barred, but this fragments and is difficult to describe by mid-body.

Habitat and Range: Timor pythons reputedly occur in open grasslands and open tropical forests of the islands of Timor and Flores.

Size: Timor pythons are a small, rather slender species. They are adult at some six feet in total length.

Breeding: In truth, there have been few Timor pythons available to zoos and hobbyists in the United States. It is not surprising, then, that the species has been successfully bred only a few times in captivity. Dallas Zoo was the first zoo to succeed. Dallas' success was followed by that of a few hobbyists. The eggs are large and the clutches average eight eggs. In North America, clutches are laid from April to June, and incubation took 64 days at 90°F (32°C). Hatchlings are large, about 16" (41 cm), a bit large for a parent six feet long or less.

Their high cost (often upwards of $1,000) and infrequent availability in the pet trade assures that only the most dedicated of hobbyists will be working with Timor pythons in the foreseeable future.

The pretty Timor python is of moderate size and only occasionally available.

Despite the fact that many people keep and breed pythons, there are no "pythons only" clubs or societies. However, among the members of most herpetological societies are usually one or two individuals with a serious interest in these snakes.

To find your local herpetological society, ask biology teachers or professors, museum curators, the naturalists at your area nature center, or the staff at pet stores.

Amateur Herpetological Societies

Arizona Herpetological Association
P.O. Box 64531
Phoenix, AZ 85082-4531
Phone: (480) 894-1625
E-mail: info@azreptiles.com

Central Florida Herpetological Society
P.O. Box 5350
Winter Park, FL 32793
www.cfhs.com/index.htm

East Texas Herpetological Society
P.O. Box 19054
Houston, TX 77224-9054
www.eths.org

North Carolina Herpetological Society
NC State Museum of Natural Sciences
11 West Jones Street
Raleigh, NC 27601-1029
www.ncherps.org

Northern California Herpetological Society
(NCHS)
P.O. Box 661738
Sacramento, CA 95866-1738
www.norcalherp.com/pages

Northern Ohio Association of Herpetologists
(NOAH)
P.O. Box 326
Columbia Station, OH 44028
www.noahonline.info/pages/aboutnoah.shtm/

Professional Herpetological Societies

Herpetologist's League
c/o Texas Natural Heritage Program
Texas Parks and Wildlife Department
4200 Smith School Road
Austin, TX 78744

Society for the Study of Amphibians
and Reptiles
Department of Zoology
Miami University
Oxford, OH 45056

Magazines

Reptiles Magazine
P.O. Box 6050
Mission Viejo, CA 92690

Reptilian Magazine
22 Firs Close
Hazlemere, High Wycombe
Bucks HP15 7TF, England

Pythons Online

www.ChicagoHerp.org

www.Faunaclassified.com

www.Kingsnake.com

Long considered the only New World python (and still often advertised as such) Loxocemus bicolor *is now thought by most systematists to be the sole member of the family Loxocemidae and is referred to as a sunbeam snake.*

About the Authors

Patricia Bartlett is an historian/naturalist who spent her early years catching almost every type of reptile she could find on the mesas near Albuquerque, New Mexico. After receiving her B.S. degree she moved to Florida to work for Ross Allen, a Florida herpetologist who opened what later became Silver Springs Resort. Bartlett has worked as an editor, writer, museum director, and data analyst. She has observed reptiles and amphibians in the field for 30 years, and has written or co-authored 53 books on their identification or captive care.

Ernie Wagner worked for Woodland Park Zoo in Seattle for 25 years, starting as a pony leader and ending up as Curator of Reptiles. Along the way came a great deal of experience with birds and mammals, but even more specifically with reptiles. He has given a wide variety of lectures on reptile behavior and published over two dozen papers on various aspects of breeding and husbandry. He owned and operated Poikilotherm Farms, a private reptile breeding facility, and has been a regular contributor to *Reptiles* magazine, on the care and breeding of reptiles.

Albino Lacking black pigment.

Ambient temperature The temperature of the air in the surrounding environment.

Anterior Towards the front.

Anus The external opening of the cloaca; the vent.

Arboreal Tree-dwelling.

Brille The transparent "spectacle" covering the eyes of a snake.

Caudal Pertaining to the tail.

cb/cb Captive bred, captive born.

cb/ch Captive bred, captive hatched.

Cloaca The common chamber into which digestive, urinary, and reproductive systems empty and which itself opens exteriorly through the vent or anus.

Constricting To wrap tightly in coils and squeeze.

Convergent evolution Evolution of two unrelated species as the result of environmental (or other) conditions.

Crepuscular Active at dusk and/or dawn.

Deposition As used here, the laying of the eggs or birthing of young.

Deposition site The spot chosen by the female to lay her eggs or have young.

Dimorphic A difference in form, build, or coloration involving the same species; often sex-linked.

Diurnal Active in the daytime.

Dorsal Pertaining to the back; upper surface.

Dorsolateral Pertaining to the upper sides.

Dorsum The upper surface.

Ecological niche The precise habitat utilized by a species.

Ectothermic "Cold-blooded."

Endothermic "Warm-blooded."

Form An identifiable species or subspecies.

Fossorial Adapted for burrowing. A burrowing species.

Genus A taxonomic classification of a group of species having similar characteristics. The genus falls between the next higher designation of "family" and the next lower designation of "species." Genera is the plural of genus. It is always capitalized when written.

Glottis The opening of the windpipe.

Gravid The reptilian equivalent of mammalian pregnancy.

Gular Pertaining to the throat.

Heliothermic Pertaining to a species which basks in the sun to thermoregulate.

Hemipenes The dual copulatory organs of male lizards and snakes.

Hemipenis The singular form of hemipenes.

Herpetoculture The captive breeding of reptiles and amphibians.

Herpetoculturist One who engages in herpetoculture.

Herpetologist One who engages in herpetology.

Herpetology The study (often scientifically oriented) of reptiles and amphibians.

Hibernacula Winter dens.

Hybrid Offspring resulting from the breeding of two species.

Hydrate To restore body moisture by drinking or absorption.

Insular As used here, island-dwelling.

Intergrade Offspring resulting from the breeding of two subspecies.

Jacobson's organs Highly enervated olfactory pits in the palate of snakes and lizards.

Juvenile A young or immature specimen.

Keel A ridge (along the center of a scale).

Labial Pertaining to the lips.

Lateral Pertaining to the side.

Melanism A profusion of black pigment.

Mental The scale at the tip of the lower lip.

Middorsal Pertaining to the middle of the back.

Midventral Pertaining to the center of the belly or abdomen.

Monotypic Containing only one type.

Nocturnal Active at night.

Ontogenetic Age-related (color) changes.

Oviparous Reproducing by means of eggs that hatch after laying.

Ovoviviparous Reproducing by means of shelled or membrane-contained eggs that hatch prior to or at deposition.

Photoperiod The daily/seasonally variable length of the hours of daylight.

Poikilothermic A species with no internal body temperature regulation. The old term was "cold-blooded."

Postocular To the rear of the eye.

Prehensile Adapted for grasping.

Prey imprinting Preferring prey of only a particular species and/or color.

Race A subspecies.

Rostral The (often modified) scale on the tip of the snout.

Rugose Not smooth. Wrinkled or tuberculate.

Saxicolous Rock-dwelling.

Scute Scale.

Species A group of similar creatures that produce viable young when breeding. The taxonomic designation which falls beneath "genus" and above "subspecies." Abbreviated as "sp."

Subspecies The subdivision of a species. A race that may differ slightly in color, size, scalation, or other criteria. Abbreviated "ssp."

Sympatric Occurring together.

Taxonomy The science of classification of plants and animals.

Terrestrial Land-dwelling.

Thermoreceptive Sensitive to heat.

Thermoregulate To regulate (body) temperature by choosing a warmer or cooler environment.

Thigmothermic Pertaining to a species (often nocturnal) which thermoregulates by being in contact with a preheated surface such as a sun-warmed boulder or tarred road surface.

Vent The external opening of the cloaca; the anus.

Venter The underside of a creature; the belly.

Ventral Pertaining to the undersurface or belly.

Ventrolateral Pertaining to the sides of the venter (= belly).

Beautiful in its normal green coloration, color variants of the green tree python (such as this yellow example) command premium prices.

Acknowledgments

We would like to acknowledge these individuals whose expertise and generosity have made this book possible, the python breeders. Forty years ago, nobody bred pythons, and the lack of knowledge was dismissed with, "There are plenty of them out there—who needs to breed them?" For some species, changing and diminishing habitats and vastly increased legislation have decreased the number imported. For other species, like the ball pythons, the demand has vastly increased, driving the development of husbandry techniques. Far-sighted individuals such as Eugene Bessette, Tracy and David Barker, John Meltzer, Regis Opferman, and Trooper Walsh looked ahead and made plans to propagate these fascinating snakes. And they've shared their knowledge with others, increasing interest in the snakes as a whole and in pythons in particular. They deserve our thanks and our support in their endeavors.

Important Note

The subject of this book is the keeping and care of nonpoisonous snakes. Snake keepers should realize, however, that even the bite of a snake regarded as nonpoisonous can have harmful consequences. So see a doctor immediately after any snake bite.

Handling giant serpents requires a lot of experience and a great sense of responsibility. Carelessness can be deadly! Inexperienced snake keepers and snake keepers who have small children are therefore urgently advised not to keep giant serpents.

Electrical appliances used in the care of snakes must carry a valid "UL approved" marking. Everyone using such equipment should be aware of the dangers involved with it. It is strongly recommended that you purchase a device that will instantly shut off the electrical current in the event of failure in the appliances or wiring. A circuit-protection device with a similar function has to be installed by a licensed electrician.

Photo Credits

All photos by Patricia Bartlett except for the following: Gerry Bucsis and Barbara Somerville: pages 26, 27, 36, and 58; cagesbydesign.com: pages 19 and 23; habitatsystemsltd.com: page 22.

Cover Photos

Patricia Bartlett: front cover, back cover, inside front cover, inside back cover.

All inquiries should be addressed to:
Barron's Educational Series, Inc.
250 Wireless Boulevard
Hauppauge, NY 11788
www.barronseduc.com

Library of Congress Catalog Card No. 2009010383

ISBN-13: 978-0-7641-4244-4
ISBN-10: 0-7641-4244-5

Library of Congress Cataloging-in-Publication Data
Bartlett, Patricia Pope, 1949– .
    Pythons / Patricia Bartlett, Ernie Wagner. — 2nd ed.
        p. cm.
    Includes bibliographical references and index.
    ISBN-13: 978-0-7641-4244-4
    ISBN-10: 0-7641-4244-5
    1. Pythons as pets. I. Wagner, Ernie. II. Title

SF459.S5B359   2009
639.3′9678—dc22   *2009010383*

Printed in China
9 8 7 6 5 4 3 2 1